BEES, BIRDS AND BUTTERFLIES
in Lace

Edna Sutton and Mary Moseley

B.T. Batsford Limited · London

ACKNOWLEDGEMENTS

We should like to express our gratitude to all those who
assisted us in the production of this book. In particular, to
those who translated the many letters to the various
consulates, and to those consulates who gave permission to
reproduce the following stamps: Royal Mail Letters, 1985
special insect stamps, bee, dragonfly and ladybird; Régie des
Postes Belges, 1981 cultural issue, owl, designed by the late
Monsieur Severin; Ministere des Transports et des
Communications, Rwanda, 1980, 50c, crake; Royal
Norwegian Embassy, London, 1981 birds K1.50, Atlantic
puffin, painted by Mr Viggo Ree; Embajada de Nicaragua,
1981 birds, 6 cor, blue-crowned motmot; Le Ministre des
Postes et Télécommunications et de l'Espace, Paris, 1962,
30c, Gallic cock; Hong Kong Post Office, Hong Kong, 1979,
HK$2, butterfly; Administration Centrale des Postes et
Télécommunications de Hongrie, Budapest, 1959, 20 fl.
butterfly and 1959, 30 fl. moth. We should also like to
thank Caphco Ltd, who advised us where to write for
permission to print the stamps we wished to use in the lace
designs in this book; Christine Corner for reading the script;
Eileen Pullan for working the needle lace and Brussels tape
lace; Edith Metcalfe, who worked the crocheted ladybird
and owl and the tatted Australian butterfly; and Kenneth
Sutton for his patient work photographing all the pieces of
lace.

First published 1991

A catalogue record for this
book is available from the
British Library.

ISBN 0 7134 6365 1

Typeset by Servis Filmsetting Ltd, Manchester

and printed in Great Britain by
Butler and Tanner Ltd, Frome, Somerset

for the Publisher
B.T. Batsford Ltd
4 Fitzhardinge Street
London W1H 0AH

CONTENTS

Note: some of the designs found in this book are large and detailed. To photograph the complete design would not show the fine detail of the stitchery and threads. 'Cut-offs' must be accepted in order to show the detail for the lacemaker. Many of the designs are repeated and enlarged, either in the colour section (between p. 66 and 67) or at the back of the book (Figs 90, 95, 109, 131 and 186)

INTRODUCTION

The techniques of the traditional English laces, and now those of the continental laces, are known and practised. Lacemakers like to use these techniques in modern designs based upon simple shapes. As experience is gained, more elaborate shapes can be developed. With this in mind, we turned to our stamp collections for inspiration. The collections specialize in butterflies, birds and crafts, from which we selected some of the designs found in this book.

The designs have been divided into three chapters, so that the simpler shapes are worked first. A variety of laces has been introduced and several threads, textures and colours suggested for working them. Each design uses one shape adapted for several laces, including: torchon, Binche, Valenciennes, Duchesse, Russian tape, Bruges flower, needle, Brussels, and Irish. Diagrams, rather than long and detailed explanations, have been used to facilitate the tasks.

We hope that this book will encourage lacemakers to design their own lace and produce individual and personal designs.

ABBREVIATIONS

LH ...   left hand
RH ...   right hand
RS ....   right side
WS ..   wrong side
cl st ..   cloth stitch
h st ...   half stitch
d st ...   double stitch (whole stitch and twist)
b st ...   back stitch
ch st .   chain stitch
tr (c) .   treble (crochet)
d c ....   double crochet
r ....   ring
p ......   picot
RW ..   reverse work
cl r ...   close ring
ch .....   chain
sl st ..   slip stitch

BEES, DRAGONFLIES AND LADYBIRDS

The bee, the dragonfly and the ladybird, each one simple in shape, have been selected here to show how they are developed and used in lacemaking. Specific threads have been suggested, but this does not mean that others may not be used. Experiment with other threads and textures.

This chapter contains several well-known laces and shows how their simple techniques are used to work the various insect shapes. The techniques can, of course, be changed to suit the individual lacemaker's requirements. This will, we hope, encourage the inexperienced lacemaker to take another simple insect shape, try several techniques, threads, textures and colours, complete a design, and work a piece of lace of her own making.

1 · BEE
torchon lace

USE: a box lid

THREADS: DMC Retors d'Alsace/Broder Machine No. 50, gold, brown, pale pink; Madeira No. 50, in white translucent

TECHNIQUES
D st edge braid (h st), hanging in a pair (cl st and h st), throwing out a pair (cl st and h st), rib with picots, setting up a straight edge, leaf plait, sewing in a pair, sewing in two pairs.

ORDER OF WORK
1 Along a line at (a) in Fig. 2 put up four pins. Using the white thread, hang on three pairs and one pair of workers at the RH edge. At this edge work a d st edge (Fig. 72) and work across in h st, finishing with a d st edge.
2 Hang in three more pairs, preparing each pair for h st (one twist on each pair). Continue to work the wing in h st, hanging

1 The bee using coloured threads, the design based upon an English stamp (see colour section)

7

in one pair at the RH side on the next two alternate rows (nine pairs on the pillow).

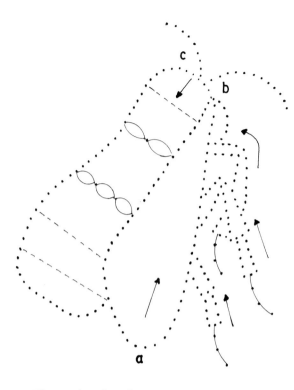

2 The torchon lace bee

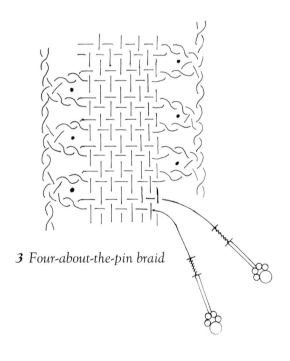

3 Four-about-the-pin braid

3 On the next row, hang in one pair of pale pink at the RH side and one pair of brown at the LH side. Hang in one pair of white on each alternate row until 14 pairs are on the pillow.

4 When the wing decreases in width throw out one pair on each alternate row. Do not throw out the pink or brown pairs just yet. Throw out a white pair at the LH edge instead.

5 The last few rows may be worked in cl st until three pairs remain. When the last pin has been worked, lay these three pairs between the last pair thrown out. Tie them close to the lace and cut them off. Using a reef knot, tie off the pairs previously thrown out and cut them off close to the lace.

The eye
1 Using the brown thread and following Fig. 4, sew four pairs into the last loop of the wing at (b) in Fig. 2.

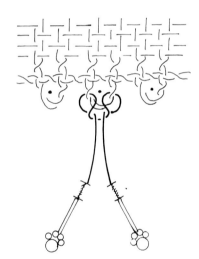

4 Sewing in a pair of bobbins

2 Work the eye in cl st, sewing into the pinloops of the wing, and work the straight edge at the RH side. Sew out, tie and cut off the threads.

The body
1 Along the line at (c) put up five pins. Using gold thread hang on two pairs on each pin. Hang in one pair, brown thread, into a central thread to act as workers.

2 Work in cl st right to left, two twists on the worker pair. Put up a pin under the workers and return to the right in cl st. Sew into the pinloop edge of the wing. Work in this manner, hanging in one pair on the next two rows on the LH side (13 pairs).

3 Work down to the line indicating where the workers are changed to gold thread (see p. 8).

4 Complete the body, working alternately in brown and gold. The last section is worked with white workers. Tie off the threads in pairs, using the pins as a support.

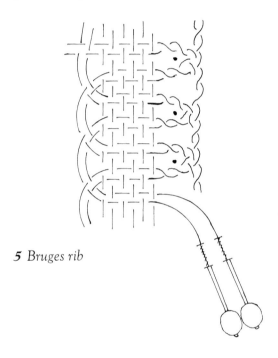

5 Bruges rib

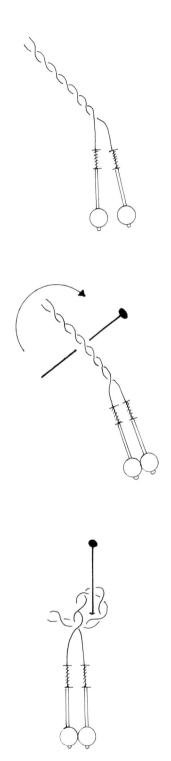

5 Work the antennae in Bruges rib with a picot (Figs. 5 and 6) to replace edge.

6 Work the legs using brown threads, as described for the Duchesse bee (p. 11). The last section includes one white pair in the plait. Sew out and tie off the threads.

7 Leaf plaits are worked in brown thread and sewn into place when the lace has been taken off the pillow.

6 Duchesse picot

2 · BEE
Duchesse lace

USE: a mirror

THREAD: Egyptian Cotton No. 60

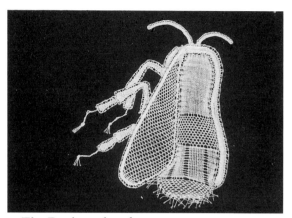

7 The Duchesse lace bee

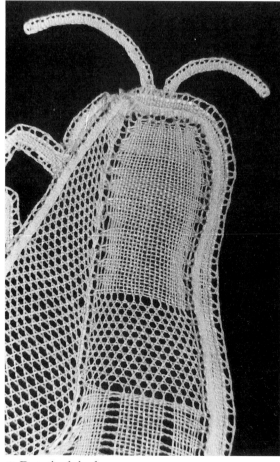

8 Detail of the bee

TECHNIQUES

Bruges rib, cl st, h st, sewing into a raised edge, hanging in a pair in h st, throwing out a pair in h st, setting up a curved edge, ladder vein.

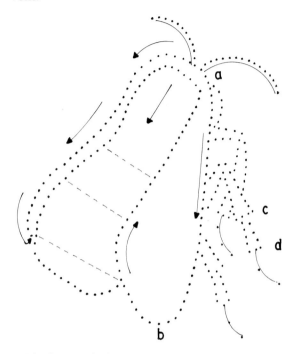

9 The bee worked in Duchesse lace

ORDER OF WORK

1 Start by working the raised edge of the wing in Bruges rib (Fig. 5) and at (a) (Fig. 9) put up a pin and hang on five pairs of bobbins. At the rear of the work put up a pin, suspend and place the contour pair (a thick and a thin thread) in position (Fig. 10).

2 Work the rib, leaving out one pair on the last two pins, before four more pairs are added (Fig. 10) in order to turn the curve.

3 From (b), h st is worked, sewing into the bottom bar of each pinloop. One pair should be hung in (Fig. 10) in each alternate row at the RH side (14 pairs on the pillow). As the wing narrows, throw out one pair at the RH side on each fifth row until 11 pairs remain. A b st, using both bars, may be used if necessary on every second row until six pairs remain. Use a reef knot to tie off each thrown-out pair.

4 Sew out only the remaining pairs into the setting-up pin.

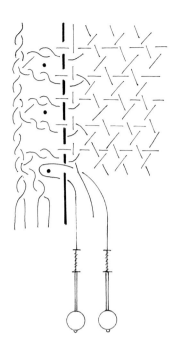

10 Hanging in a pair, h st braid

5 Using these six pairs (including the contour pair), work the rib down the RH edge of the narrow strip (the eye) by rolling and sewing into the edge of the wing.
6 Turn the top section of the wing as shown in Fig. 11. Work in cl st. Sew into the lower bar of the raised edge and work a straight edge on the outer edge.

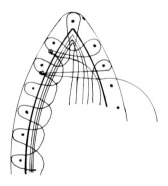

11 Turning the top section for raised work

7 Sew out into the wing and tie and cut off the threads.
8 At the top of the body (inside the LH edge of the wing), sew in 15 pairs. Work in cl st, sewing into the pinloop at each side. It will be necessary to hang in one pair to accommodate the curve at the LH side. As the shape of the curve changes, throw out one or two pairs at the LH side. Separate this section by adding one extra twist on all passive threads.
9 Work the second section in h st.
10 The third section is divided by using a 'ladder', twists on the worker threads. Add further pairs at the RH edge.
11 The last section is worked in h st. As this section is worked, tie off one pair at each pin around the curved edge. Work the edge as two twists about the pin. Leave a 3 mm fringe from each pin at the lower edge. Work the antennae in Bruges rib (Fig. 5).

The legs
1 Along the line at (c) set up the straight edge (Fig. 12), using ten pairs and one contour pair.

12 Setting up a straight edge (four-about-the pin edge)

2 Work the centre section in cl st, throwing out two pairs on each row until five pairs remain. Turn the corner and work the top section, sewing into the wing. Throw out pairs, leaving three pairs to sew out into the wing. Tie and cut off the threads.
3 Along the line at (d) set up the straight edge in a similar way, sewing out and tying off into the centre section. Work the plait.
4 The other legs are worked in the same way.

3 · BEE
Irish lace

USE: a lavender bag

THREADS AND MATERIALS: DMC Retors d'Alsace/Broder Machine Nos 30 and 50, DMC Coton Perlé No. 12, organdie, coarse tulle, a hemmed 40 × 40 cm piece of cotton (cover cloth), architect's paper

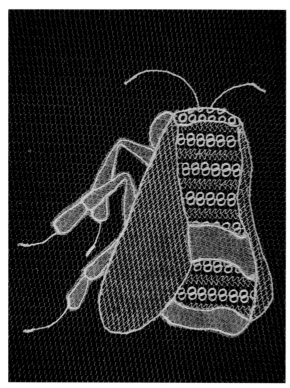

13 The bee worked in Irish lace

TECHNIQUES
Couching, Irish lace filling No. 1 and No. 5.

PREPARATION
1 Iron the cover cloth, tulle and organdie.
2 In felt-tip, trace the design on to the paper.
3 Place the cover cloth flat on the table. Pin and tack the traced design to it, ink side down (Fig. 14).
4 Place the tulle and then the organdie on top of the cloth and design (Fig. 15), and tack the four layers together.
5 Tack close to each part of the design so that all the layers are held together firmly.

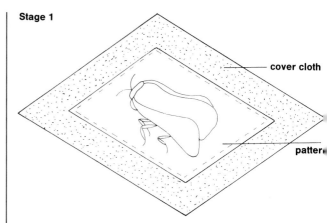

Stage 1

cover cloth

pattern

14 Pin and tack together the cover cloth and traced design

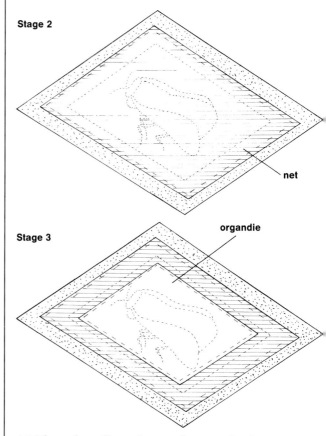

Stage 2

net

Stage 3

organdie

15 Place the tulle and organdie over the design; tack

ORDER OF WORK
1 Refer to Fig. 13 to see which sections are worked in organdie and which are worked in stitchery. The organdie sections are worked first.

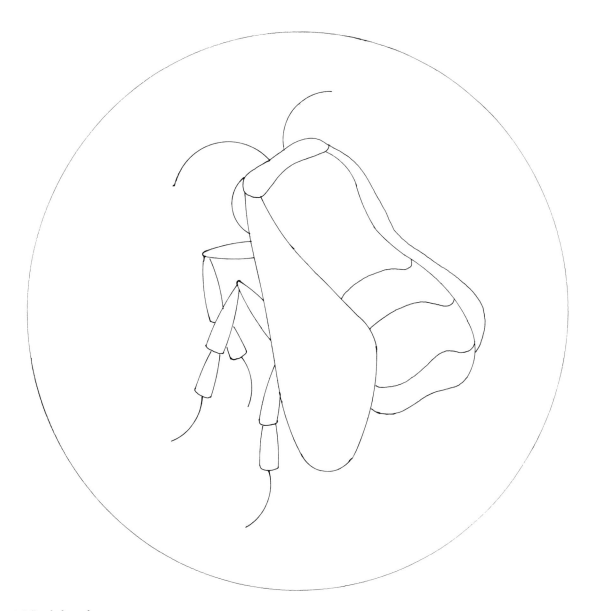

16 Irish lace bee

2 Following Fig. 17, work the couching, using DMC Retors d'Alsace/Broder Machine No. 50, around the eye, the legs, and the two sections of the body. Thread the Coton Perlé into a needle and pass the needle through to the WS. Leave just 2 cm on the WS and a longer length on the RS. Start and finish the finer thread on the RS, with a b st over the thicker thread and through both layers of fabric.

3 Remove the tacking threads around the bee and cut away the unwanted organdie. The tulle remains uncut.

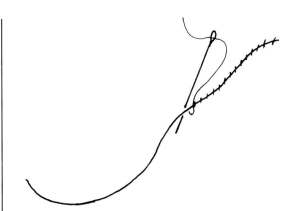

17 Couching over the design lines

4 Tack the fabrics together close to the unworked design and complete the couching over the remaining lines of the design.

5 Work Irish lace filling No. 1 (Fig. 18) in the wings, and Irish lace filling No. 5 (Fig. 19) in the body. Care must be taken to rejoin new threads in the couched threads only, and not in the middle of a line of the filling.

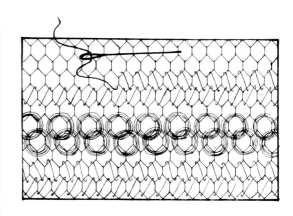

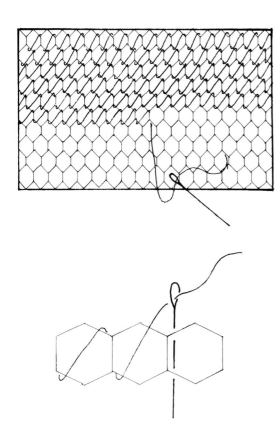

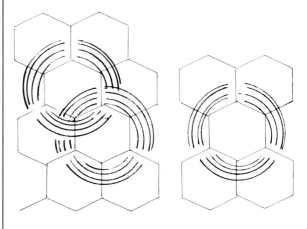

19 Irish lace filling No. 5

18 Irish lace filling No. 1

COMPLETION

1 Carefully remove all the tacking threads and separate the design from the fabrics.

2 The thicker threads which have been left on the WS must be fastened securely to those on the RS.

3 Working from the WS, turn each thread back over itself and using a needle and thread overcast the two together for 2 cm. Cut off both threads close to the fabric.

4 When all the threads are secured, the lace, protected by a linen cloth, must be pressed on the WS with a moderately hot iron.

4 · BEE
needle lace

USE: a picture

THREADS: Cordonnet, 40/3 Gütermann silk; stitches, 100/3 Gütermann silk; cordonnette of four threads 40/3, buttonholed in 100/3 Gütermann silk

TECHNIQUES
Single Brussels, pea stitch and variations, corded single Brussels, corded treble Brussels, inverted pyramid.

PREPARATION
1 Trace the design on to a piece of architect's paper, using a felt-tipped pen.
2 Fold a large cover cloth into four. Place the design ink side down on top of the folded cover cloth and tack them together.

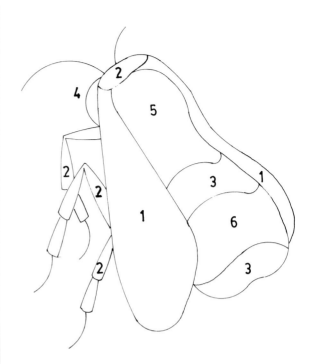

22 The bee worked in needle lace

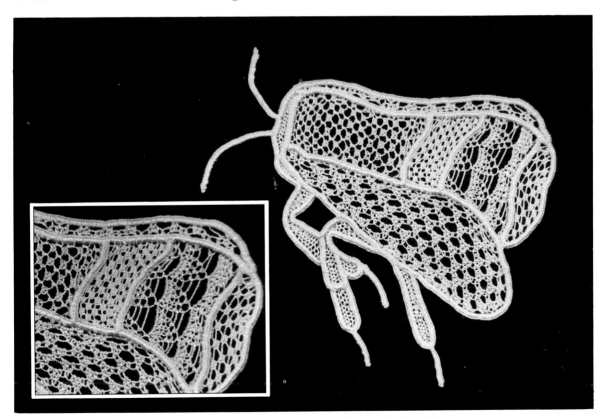

20 Detail of the needle lace bee, showing a variety of stitches

21 The needle lace bee

15

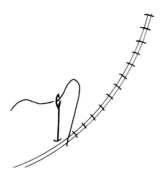

23 *Laying the cordonnet*

1 Follow Fig. 23; using 40/3 silk, couch the cordonnet (two threads) along all the lines. Where lines meet it may be necessary to take one thread down and return the thread to make a pair of threads. Continue as before.
2 The couching threads go through to the WS. These threads are usually 2 mm apart.

Foundation row

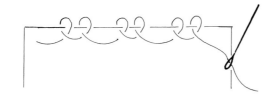

Stage 1

Stage 2

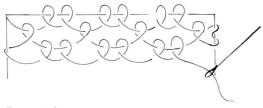

24 *Pea stitch*

Foundation row

Stage 1

25 *Single Brussels*

16

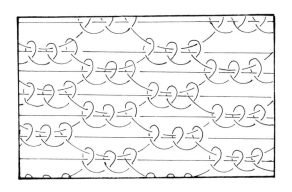

Foundation row

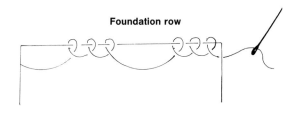

Stage 1

Stage 1

Stage 2

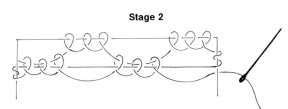

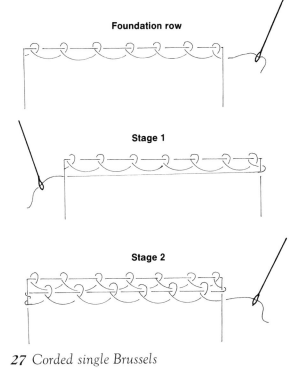

26 *Corded treble Brussels*

27 *Corded single Brussels*

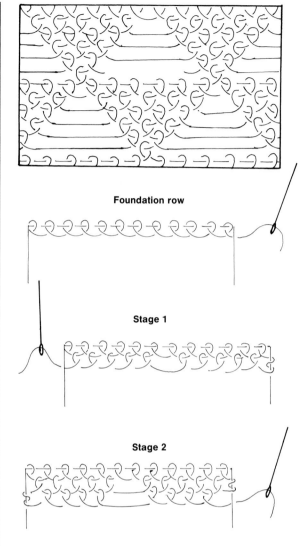

Foundation row

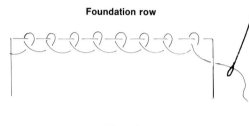

Stage 1

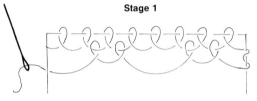

Stage 2

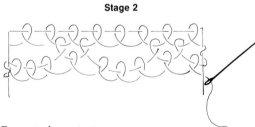

28 Pea stitch variation

29 Inverted pyramid

**Continue working rows 3, 4, 5 by
reducing 1 stitch on each row.
Next batch of Pyramids are worked
into spaces**

3 The areas are marked numerically for identification of the stitches:
(1) pea stitch variation (Fig. 24);
(2) single Brussels (Fig. 25);
(3) corded treble Brussels (Fig. 26);
(4) corded single Brussels (Fig. 27);
(5) Pea stitch variation (Fig. 28);
(6) inverted pyramid (Fig. 29).
4 When all the filling stitches have been worked work the final edging, the cordonnette (Fig. 30).

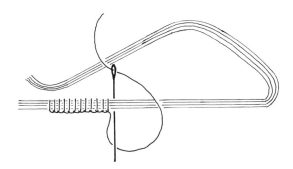

30 Working the cordonette

5 Using four threads of 40/3 silk for the cordonnette and 100/3 silk in the needle, work around the edges of the design in buttonhole stitch. Take care to (a) pick up a little of the stitches already worked; (b) cover the four threads at the same time with the buttonhole stitches.
6 Keep a good tension throughout, ensuring the stitches are all the same size, and keep the fastening off and joins as neat as possible.
7 Remove the design from the cover cloth by snipping or pulling the two apart.
8 Snip off any remaining threads and press carefully on the WS.

5 · DRAGONFLY
Duchesse lace

USE: a picture

THREADS: Egyptian Cotton No. 60, DMC Coton Perlé No. 12

31 The dragonfly worked in Duchesse lace

TECHNIQUES
Setting up a curved edge, cl st, h st, straight edge (four-about-the-pin edge) braid, h st vein, throwing out a pair, raised edge sewing, hanging in a pair, b st used in a raised edge, Bruges rib.

ORDER OF WORK
Eyes
1 At (a) (Fig. 32) put up two pins and start to set up the curved edge using cl st (Fig. 33). Eight pairs, including the contour pairs, are used to work the eyes. Gradually reduce the pairs to six.
2 Throw out the inner contour thread (thick), and one thin thread. Take the workers through all the passive threads to the centre and leave.

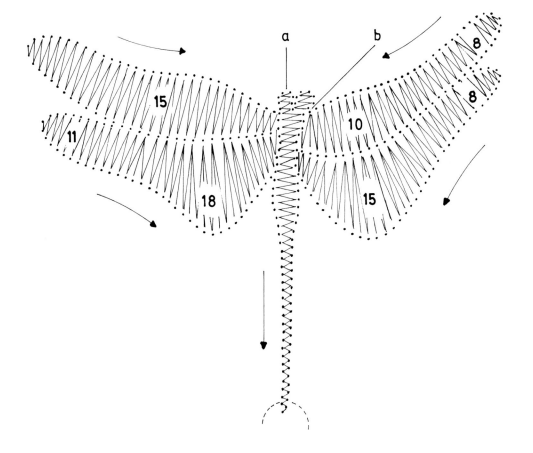

32 Duchesse lace techniques are used to work the dragonfly

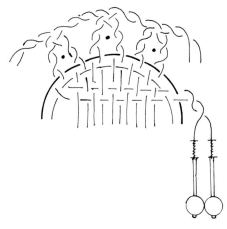

33 Duchesse lace: setting up a curved edge

3 Work the other eye in the same way, leaving the workers in the centre. Pick up the LH centre pair. Complete the row in cl st. Throw out one pair at each edge.

20

The body

1 Work the next section of the body in h st. At the waist, twist each passive pair twice more.

2 Work the shaped section in cl st, with a h st vein in the centre. The last section is worked in cl st, gradually reducing to five pairs at the last pin. Place the thick contour threads to the back, and cut off later. Leave the remaining threads as long threads. Tie in a knot when taken off the pillow. Fig. 31 shows how the thick contour threads have been used to decorate the tail.

The RH upper wing

1 At pinhole (b), at the base of the eye, sew in five pairs and hang in the contour pair. Work in rib (Fig. 5) and turn the curve as in Fig. 11. Using h st, work the upper wing, increasing first to eight pairs and finally to ten pairs.

2 Sew out into the body. Tie off these pairs only, do not cut threads at this stage.

The RH lower wing

1 Select six of these pairs and the contour pair. Cut off the unwanted pairs.
2 Sew the group of six pairs, using the seventh pair to make the sewing, along the lower edge of the top wing. Keep the group of threads straight and in the same order. Do not let them twist (Fig. 34).

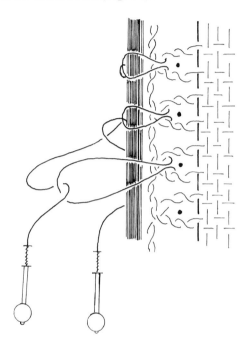

34 Working a sewn raised edge

3 Turn the curved edge as before. Work the lower wing in h st. Hang in two more pairs, and there should be nine pairs on the pillow.
4 Continue in h st. Make the sewing over the group of threads, sewing into the lower bar of the pinloop. As the wing increases in width, hang in one pair at the RH edge in each alternate row. As the wing narrows, throw out one pair at the RH edge until eight pairs remain. Sew out, tie securely and cut off the threads.

The LH wings

1 Reverse the working of the raised edge to the LH edge of the upper wing. Turn the curve and work in h st. Hang in the two pairs as indicated and complete the wings. Reverse the instructions regarding the direction in which the ribs are worked.

6 · DRAGONFLY
Brussels tape lace

USE: a child's dress

THREADS AND MATERIALS: DMC Special Dentelles, 1 m narrow Brussels lace tape, architect's paper, cover cloth

35 The dragonfly worked in Brussels tape lace

TECHNIQUES
Russian stitch, twisted Russian stitch, eight-thread twisted wheel.

PREPARATION
1 Trace the design on to a piece of architect's paper with a felt-tipped pen. Tack the design ink side down on to a folded cover cloth.
2 Press the tape, and gather up one of the edges along the length of tape. Use the special thread woven into each edge. When using a long length of tape snip the special thread every metre and gather up each section. Take care that the special thread is not withdrawn in error.
3 Place the prepared braid on the pattern. Pin into position, drawing up the thick thread a little more as and when needed. Make sure the braid is kept in a good shape at this stage, gathering to accommodate turns, etc. (Fig. 37).
4 Tack in position, holding both edges in place.

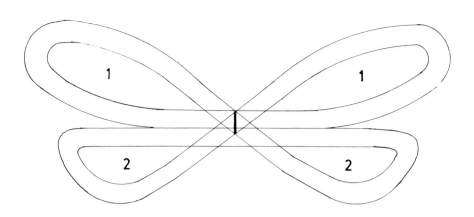

36a *Simple Brussels tape lace dragonfly, the wings*

36b *Simple Brussels tape lace dragonfly, the body*

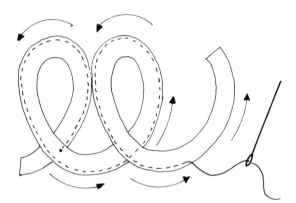

37 *Shaping and tacking Brussels tape lace*

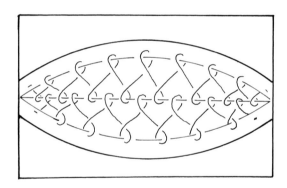

Stage 1

Stage 2

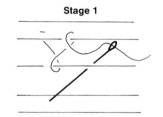

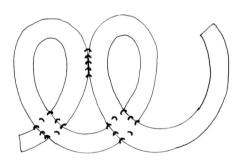

38 *Hem the tape firmly into position*

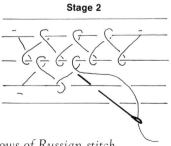

39 *Two rows of Russian stitch*

5 Curves, crossings, etc., where they touch each other, must be sewn together as neatly as possible (Fig. 38).

6 The upper side is the RS.

ORDER OF WORK

1 The spaces are now ready to be filled with decorative stitches:

(1) two rows Russian stitch (Fig. 39);

(2) twisted Russian (Fig. 40);

(3) eight-thread twisted wheel (Fig. 41).

2 Take out the tacking threads and sew the wings to the body.

3 Press on the WS, protected by a damp cloth.

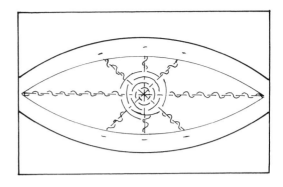

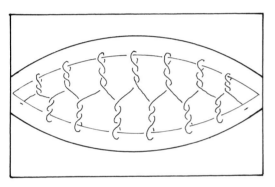

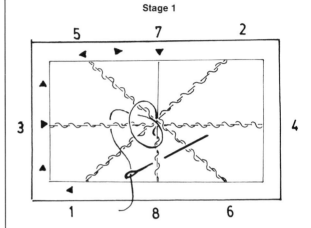

Stage 1

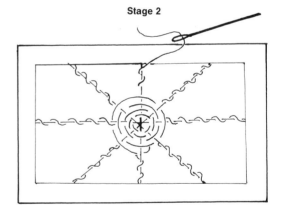

Stage 2

41 Eight-thread twisted wheel

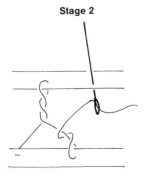

40 Twisted Russian

7 · DRAGONFLY
Irish lace

USE: a place mat

THREADS AND MATERIALS: DMC Retors d'Alsace/Broder Machine Nos 30 and 50, DMC Coton Perlé No. 12, organdie, coarse tulle, hemmed 40 × 40 cm piece of cotton fabric (cover cloth), architect's paper

TECHNIQUES
Couching, Irish lace filling Nos 1 (variation) and 3, twirling, seeds/pops.

PREPARATION
Prepare the organdie and tulle as described for the Irish lace bee (p. 12).

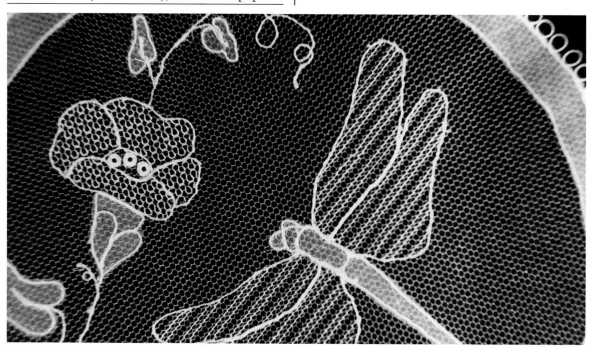

42 The dragonfly placemat, worked in Irish lace

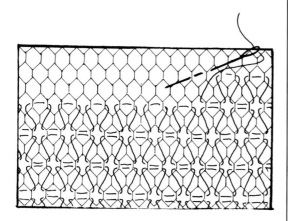

43 Irish lace filling No. 3

ORDER OF WORK
1 Refer to Fig. 42 to see which parts are worked in organdie and which in stitchery. Couch around the outer circle lines, the body, the leaves and the calyx.

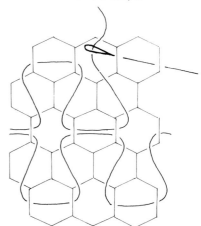

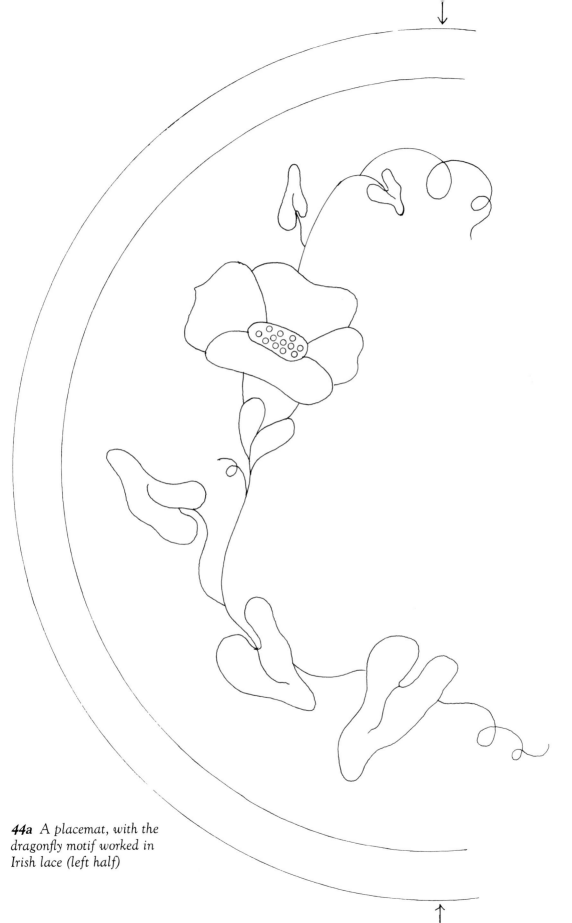

44a A placemat, with the
dragonfly motif worked in
Irish lace (left half)

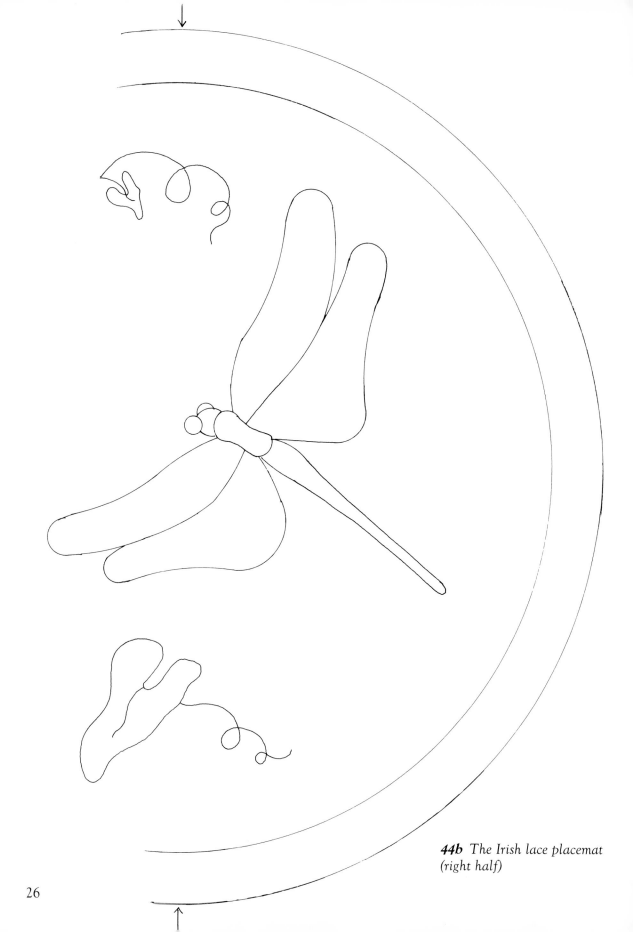

44b *The Irish lace placemat
(right half)*

2 Remove the support tacking threads. Cut away the unwanted organdie only inside the circle.
3 Tack close to the design again. Couch along the stems, the petals, and the wings.
4 Work Irish lace filling No. 1 (variation) (Fig. 18) in the wings, Irish lace filling No. 3 (Fig. 43) in the petals, and work three seeds/pops (Fig. 44) in the centre of the petals.
5 Work the twirling in Coton Perlé (Fig. 46) around the outer edge. Close to the edge cut away the organdie and tulle under the twirling.

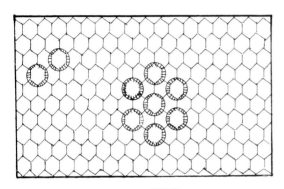

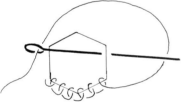

45 *Working the seeds/pops*

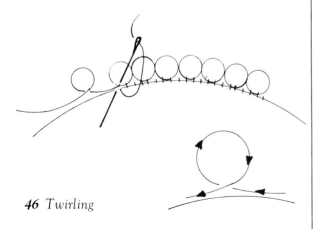

46 *Twirling*

COMPLETION
Finish off the work as described for the Irish lace bee (p. 14).

8 · DRAGONFLY
crocheted lace

USE: a workbag

THREADS: DMC Special Dentelles, variegated green, lilac and black

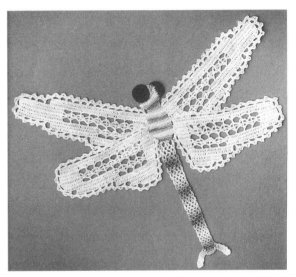

47 *The crocheted lace dragonfly*

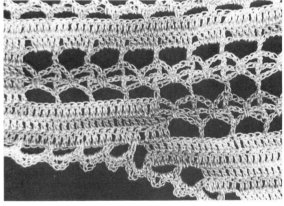

48 *A section of the crocheted wings*

TECHNIQUES
Chain (ch), double crochet (d c), treble crochet (tr), slip stitch (sl st).

ORDER OF WORK
The body
1 Refer to the chart (Fig. 49a). The body is worked upside down. Using green thread, work 13 ch st, turn and work 12 d c.

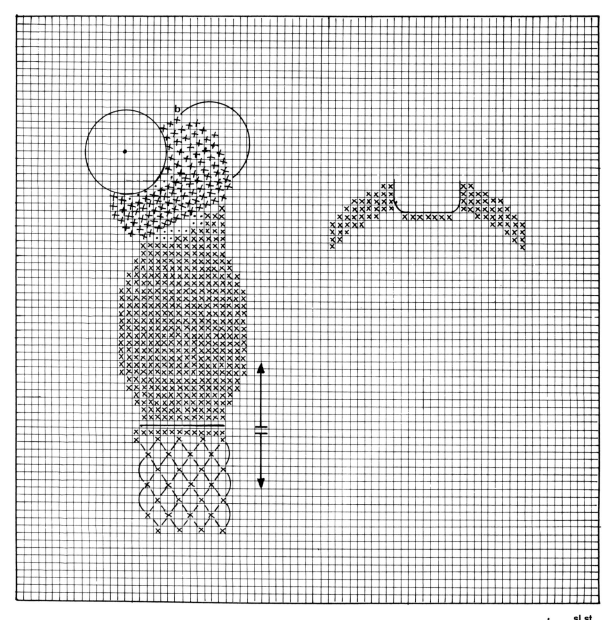

49a Body of the crocheted dragonfly

2 Follow the chart, working in d c, shaping the neck carefully. Fasten off at (b).

The round eye

1 Make a circle with two strands of the black yarn. Work eight d c about this circle of two strands.

2 Close the circle by pulling the loose end. Close the ring with a sl st.

3 *1st row*: continuing in d c, increase in every stitch (16 sts).

4 *2nd row*: d c in alternate stitches (24 sts).

5 *3rd row*: increase in every third stitch (32 sts).

6 *4th row*: work in d c. Fasten off.

The head

Using the chart as a guide, work the head. Join to the 'round' eye at the end of each alternate row.

28

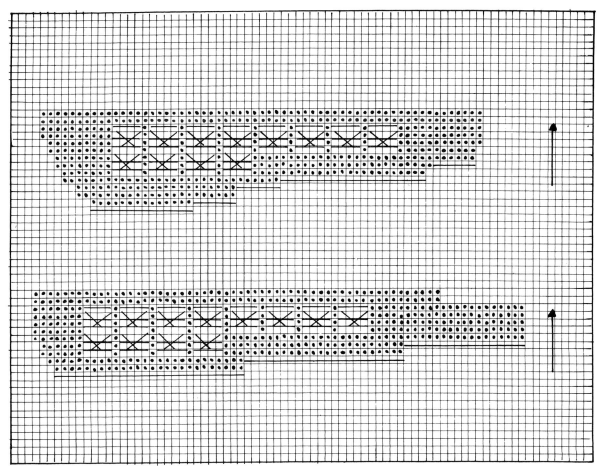

49b *Wings of the crocheted dragonfly*

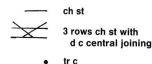

——————	ch st
$\Join$	3 rows ch st with d c central joining
●	tr c

The second eye
This eye is worked as the round eye, but in a semicircle and joined to the head at the end of each row.

The tail
The simple net ground is worked from the body down towards the tail.
1 *1st row:* 1 d c, 5 ch, miss 2 ch, 1 d c into the next ch. Repeat to the end of the row. 5 ch. Turn.
2 *2nd row:* 1 d c into 5 ch loop, 5 ch, 1 d c. Repeat to the end of the row. 5 ch. Turn.
3 Repeat these two rows six times (14 rows).
4 Change to 4 ch for 14 rows, and then to 3 ch for a further 14 rows. Fasten off.

The wings
1 Look at the chart (Fig. 49b), and note

(a) the start;
(b) the direction of working;
(c) sl sts and increasing for the next row;
(d) ch sts used for joining with a d c.

To finish the wings
1 Sew the wings to the body of the dragonfly. Starting at the inside edge of the wings, join in the thread, and work 1 d c, 5 ch, miss 4 d c, 1 d c into the next stitch. Repeat to the edge where the wings are joined to the body.
2 Turn. 2 d c, 3 ch, 2 d c into each space. Repeat to the end. Fasten off.
3 Press on the WS.

9 · LADYBIRD
torchon lace

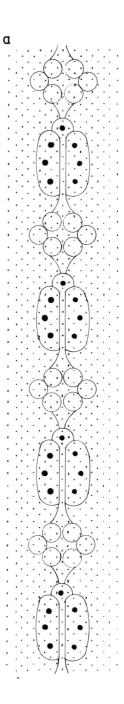

USE: decoration for a box

THREADS: DMC Retors d'Alsace/Broder Machine No. 50, white; DMC Coton Perlé No. 8, white

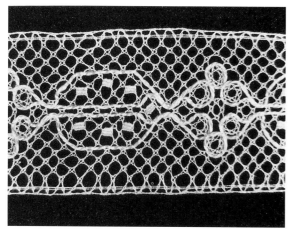

50 A hand-made box decorated with a ladybird motif worked in torchon lace

TECHNIQUES
Dieppe ground, tally, roseground, straight edge, passing a gimp.

ORDER OF WORK
1 Start to hang on 14 pairs and work the bobbins from (a) (Fig. 51). Gradually hang them on in a straight line, so as to work each diagonal line in turn.

2 Introduce the gimp threads as required, passing them through a pair of threads. When the gimp thread is passed to the right pass it under the first thread and over the second thread. When the gimp is passed to the left the gimp passes over the first thread and under the second thread.

3 Follow Fig. 51 carefully, observing Fig. 50. Notice the following:
(a) the roseground in the rings;
(b) the tallies in the ladybird;
(c) where the gimps cross, left over right.

4 It is optional to cross the inner two gimps when starting to work the head.

51 Torchon lace braid, ideal for decorating a box

10 · LADYBIRD
Brussels tape lace

USE: decoration of a large box of matches

THREADS AND TAPE: DMC Special
Dentelles, 50 cm narrow Brussels lace tape

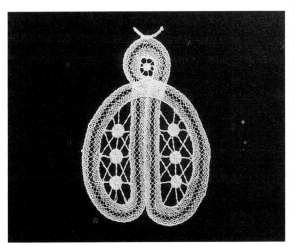

52 The Brussels tape lace ladybird

53 Detail of the Brussels tape lace ladybird

TECHNIQUES
Eight-wheel/legged spider (laid threads
twisted), couched threads which are later
buttonholed.

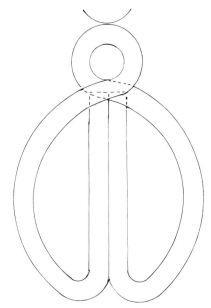

54 The Brussels tape lace ladybird motif

PREPARATION
Prepare for working as described in Brussels
lace dragonfly (p. 21).

ORDER OF WORK
1 Work one eight-wheel/legged twisted
spider in the head, and six in the body (Fig.
55).
2 For the antennae, two couched threads are
laid and then buttonholed over the top.
3 Remove all the tacking threads and press
on the WS, protecting it with a damp cloth.

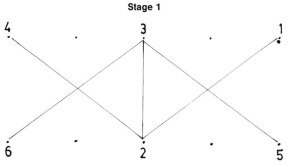

Stage 1

single threads 1, 2, 3
whip back 3 to 2
single thread 2 to 4
whip back 4, 2, 1
single threads 5, 3, 6
whip back 6, 3, 5

Stage 2

single threads 7, 8, 9, 10, 7
whip back 7, 10, 9, 8, 7

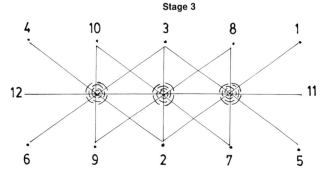

Stage 3

single thread 11 to 12, working knot where threads cross
whip back 12 to 11 working a woven spider at each crossing
  of threads

55 Eight wheel/legged spider, laid threads twisted

11 · LADYBIRD
torchon lace motif

USE: a pocket decoration

THREAD: Bouc Linen 100/2

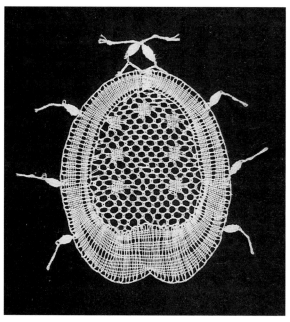

56 A torchon lace motif

TECHNIQUES
Straight edge (four-about-the-pin edge) braid, a ladder, hanging in and throwing out a pair, plaits, leaf plaits, joining several threads, torchon ground, cl st bud b. st.

ORDER OF WORK
1 Along the line at (a) (Fig. 57) put up four pins. On each pin hang on two pairs of bobbins. Carefully follow the worker line on the pricking. Starting from the outer edge, work a cl st and two twists with the outer pairs.
2 Work a straight-edge braid. Work the 'ladders' as marked. Add and throw out the three extra pairs where indicated. Take care to firm the threads after working each row.
3 Join the braid by joining the passive pairs into the setting up pinloops. One pair should be joined to one pinloop.
4 Tie and cut off the threads.

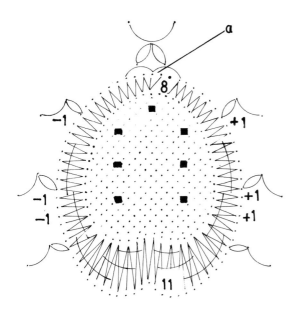

4 Sew out each pair. Firm each pair, tie and cut off the threads close to the lace.
5 Work the head and legs in leaf plaits and plaits.

57 *A simple torchon ladybird motif, originating from an English stamp*

The filling (torchon ground)
1 Sew in the appropriate pairs to the pinloops of the braid, starting at the top RH side.
2 Work the ground by twisting each pair once, cl st, pin, cl st, twist each pair once. The buds are worked in cl st (Fig. 58).

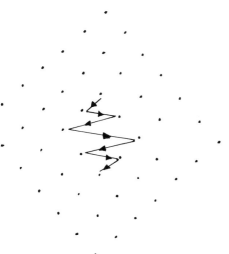

58 *Working a cl st bud*

3 The worker pairs may be sewn into the pinloops only and used again as passive pairs.

12 · LADYBIRD
Irish lace

USE: decorating a box lid

THREADS AND MATERIALS: DMC
Retors d'Alsace/Broder Machine Nos 30 and
50, DMC Coton Perlé No. 12, organdie,
coarse tulle, architect's paper, cover cloth,
ballpoint needles

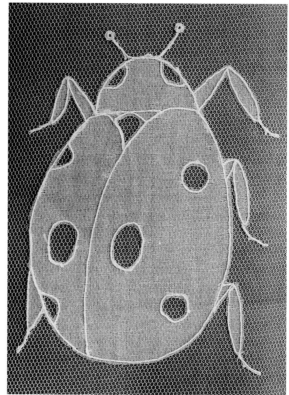

60 A hand-made box decorated with a ladybird motif worked in Irish lace

59 Irish lace ladybird used as a box lid decoration

TECHNIQUES
Couching.

PREPARATION
Prepare the organdie and tulle as described for the Irish lace bee (p. 12).

ORDER OF WORK
1 Couch around the outline, the head, the spots, and the legs.
2 Remove the tacking threads. Cut away the unwanted organdie only. Couch the antennae line and the end section of each leg.

COMPLETION
Finish off the lace as described for the Irish lace bee (p. 14).

$\mathcal{B}$IRDS

In this chapter you will find a further collection of laces, this time used in the designs of birds. A simple shape has been developed and then adapted to use English and Continental bobbin lace, needle lace, crochet and Irish lace techniques. A variety of threads have been utilized to show the effect of different textures and colours when used together.

1 · OWL
Bruges flower lace

USE: a picture

THREADS: Gütermann machine thread, shade Nos 285, 837, 979 (marked on pricking as Nos 6, 8, 10 respectively)

61 The Bruges flower lace owl

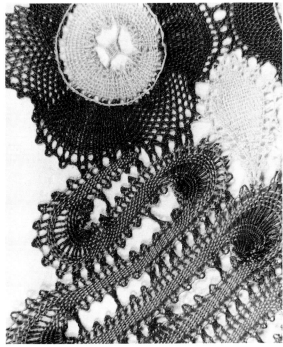

62 The Bruges flower lace owl, showing the eye, beak and wing details

TECHNIQUES
Cl st, h st, d st edge, straight edge (four-about-the-pin) braid, plait-with-picot, false plait, b st, tally, setting up a leaf, tying off several threads.

ORDER OF WORK
The inner circle (eyes)
1 Using shade No. 979, first work the inner circle. Put up three pins, and hang two pairs on each pin.

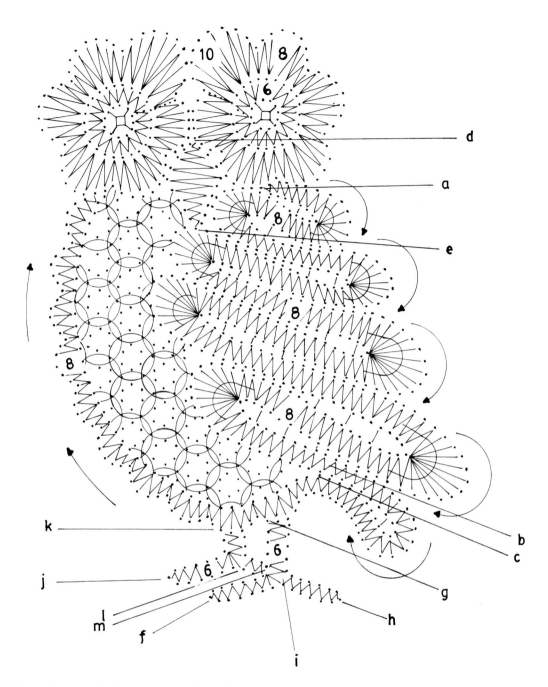

63 The owl worked in Bruges flower lace, the design based on a Belgian stamp

2 Starting at the outer edge, work cl st, two twists on each pair, and cl st towards the inner edge. Here a d st edge is worked. B sts are worked on the inner edge.
3 Follow the worker line carefully and cl st to the outer edge. Again work a four-about-the-pin edge (Fig. 3).

4 Complete the inner circle in this manner, finally taking the worker to the outer edge. Join into a circle by sewing one pair of threads into each pinloop. Tie off the threads (Fig. 64) and lay one pair close to the outer edge and to the back of the work. This pair will be used to work the petals.
5 Cut off the other pairs close to the lace.

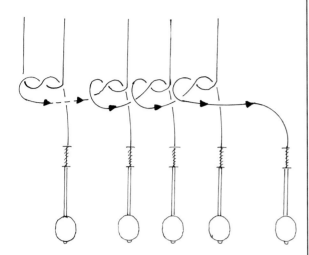

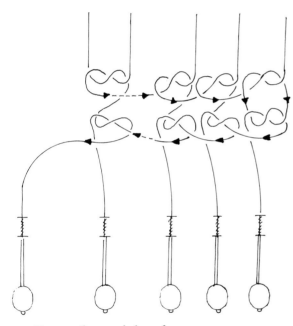

64 *Tying off several threads*

The outer petals/eyes

1 In line with the setting up of the inner circle, put up four pins.
2 Using shade No. 837, hang on seven pairs. Take up the pair from the inner circle as workers, and using cl st, work out to the edge. Work a d st edge, and return to the inner edge.

3 Remove the pin from the inner circle edge, and make a sewing into the first bar of the first pinloop (Fig. 65) close to the tying off line. Where three lines meet at one pinhole, use the second bar to act as a b st (Fig. 66). When only one sewing is worked take the crochet hook under both bars. Cross the workers before making the sewing when working cl st only. The workers are already twisted in h st. Replace the pin.

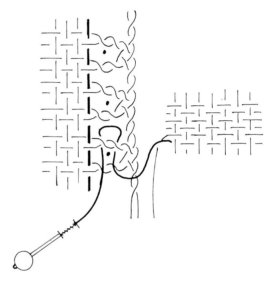

65 *Raised edge sewing using one bar, the first sewing worked in cl st or h st*

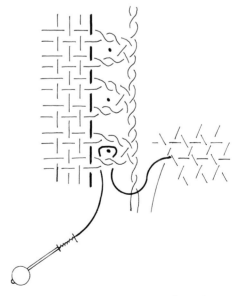

66 *Raised edge sewing using one bar, the second sewing acts as a b st*

4 Take care to curve the threads carefully around the outer edges of the petals.

5 The petals are worked alternately in cl st and h st, each petal being separated by a row of d sts worked from the outer to the inner edge.

6 In the wider petals two extra pairs may be added and then thrown out when not required.

7 Before joining the petals, twist each passive pair once. Work a row of d st and make the sewings into the starter pinloops. Tie and cut off the threads close to the lace.

The wings

1 At (a) (Fig. 63) gradually sew and hang in eight pairs of shade No. 285 and 1 pair of shade No. 837 as workers.

2 Observe Fig. 63 and you will see the 'ladder' (two twists on the worked pair) marked around the outer edge of the curve. Work a d st edge braid for the wings. Note the directional arrows.

3 False plaits are worked to join the wings together (Fig. 67).

4 Throw out one pair of passives at (b) and sew out the worker at (c). Join in the new worker pair, shade No. 285, and complete the tail and chest in h st. Sew out the pairs into the edge of the eyes. Tie and cut off the threads.

Stage 2

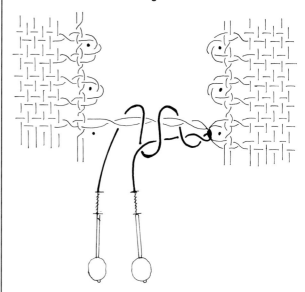

Stage 3

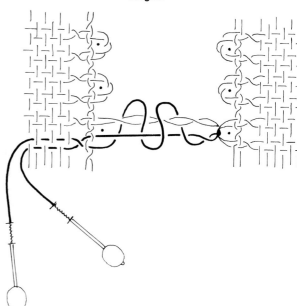

67 Stages of working a false plait

Stage 1

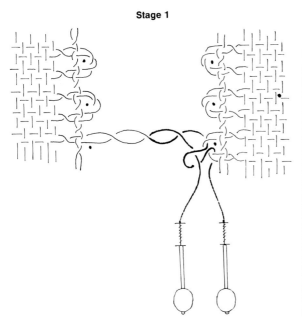

The beak

1 At (d) sew in two pairs of shade No. 979. Following Fig. 63 set up the beak as for a leaf (Fig. 68). Fourteen pairs will be needed for the beak.

2 Reduce, by throwing out pairs gradually, to two pairs and sew out at (e).

38

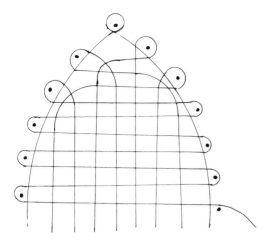

68 *Setting up a Bruges flower lace leaf*

The filling
1 Using shade No. 979, work the plait-with-picot filling (Fig. 69). Sew in and sew out the pairs carefully in order to keep the filling in good shape.

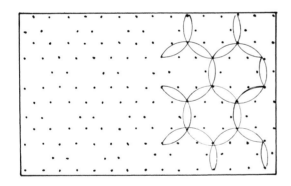

69 *Plait-with-picot filling*

The feet
1 The feet are worked in shade No. 979. Six pairs are used to work the d st edge braid. Start at (f), using the technique for setting up a leaf and sew out at (g). Work (h) to (i), (j) to (k) and (l) to (m).

2 · OWL
Russian tape lace

USE: a picture

THREADS: Gütermann machine thread shade No. 414 and gold (personal choice)

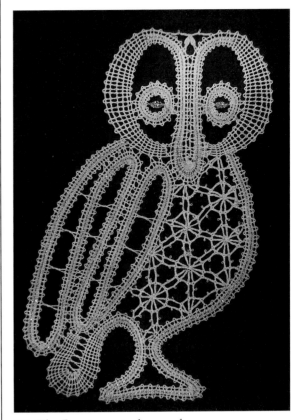

70 *The Russian tape lace owl*

TECHNIQUES
Russian tape braid (with decorative centre), cl st, d st, b st, d st edge, false plait, plait-with-picot, sewings, windmill join, pivot-on-a-pin, tying off several threads, stitch-and-twist braid, leaf plait, Russian tape lace filling.

ORDER OF WORK
1 Study Fig. 71 and note the directional arrows and the various sections and braids used in working the owl. At (a) put up three pins and hang on seven pairs in shade No. 414.

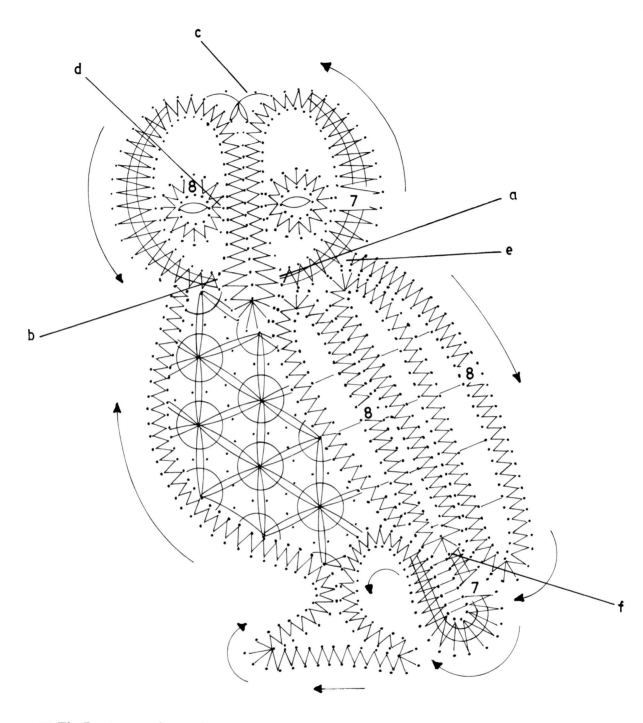

71 *The Russian tape lace owl*

2 Work in a stitch-and-twist braid (with a d st edge) (Fig. 72) until the braid narrows at the top of the head.
3 Change to Russian tape braid (Fig. 73). Working from Fig. 71, introduce the gold thread. Continue round the beak and finish using the gold thread at the top of the head at the LH side.
4 Change back to a stitch-and-twist braid as used on the RH side. Sew out all the threads at (b), tie and cut off.

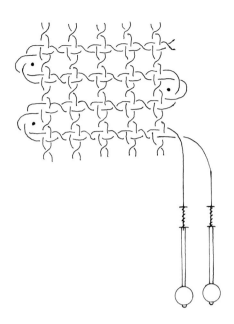

72 Stitch-and-twist/d st edge braid

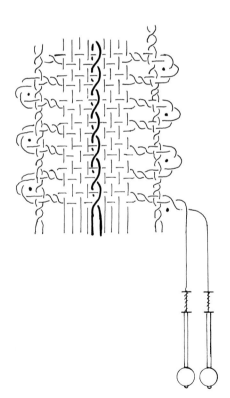

73 Russian tape lace decorative braid

5 At (c) sew in two pairs of shade No. 414 at each side of the head. Work plaits-with-picots (Fig. 74), crossing with a 'windmill'. Work the leaf plaits (Fig. 75) and sew out.

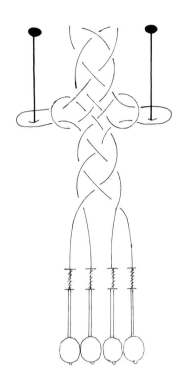

74 Plait-with-picot

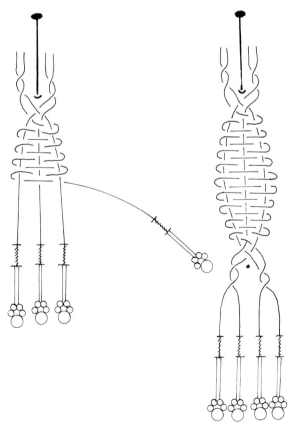

75 Leaf plait

The eyes

1 At (d) put up three pins. Using shade No. 414 hang on seven pairs and one pair of gold. Work in d st edge, cl st braid (Russian tape braid). Note the sewings into the head and beak.

2 Join the braid, tie and cut off.

3 Work the leaf plait in gold in the centre of each eye.

The wings

1 At (e) sew in seven pairs of shade No. 414 and one pair of gold. Work the Russian tape braid (Fig. 73). Note the sewings into the head, the wing braid and the false plaits. Sew out and cut off, etc.

The tail, feet and chest

1 At (f) sew in seven pairs of shade No. 414. Work the short section in a stitch-and-twist-braid, introduce the gold thread after the tail is finished and work the Russian tape braid around the feet and the chest. Sew out into the head.

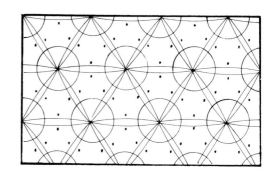

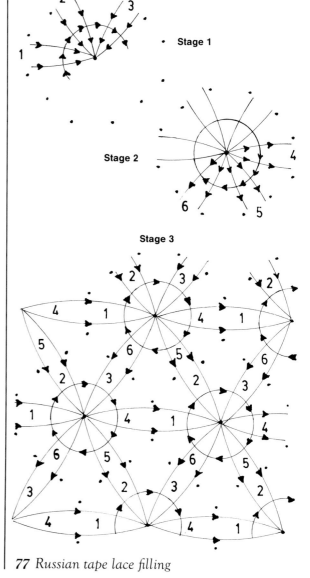

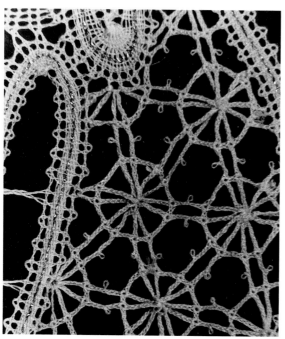

76 Detail of the Russian tape lace filling

77 Russian tape lace filling

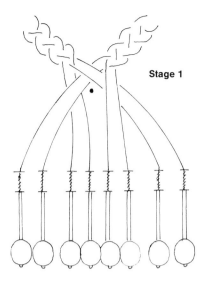

Stage 1

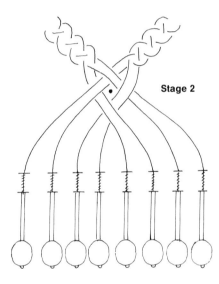

Stage 2

78 Windmill join

The chest filling
1 Great care must be taken when working this filling. Follow the numerical order (Fig. 77) when working the plaits-with-picots. Use shade No. 414, the plaits being crossed with a windmill join (Fig. 78) by first splitting all the threads into four groups.
2 Use each group as one thread to work the windmill.
3 Re-group the threads into groups of two pairs and work the plaits-with-picots in the usual way.

3 · OWL
crocheted lace

USE: a child's pinafore

THREADS: DMC Special Dentelles beige, dark brown, variegated gold/brown

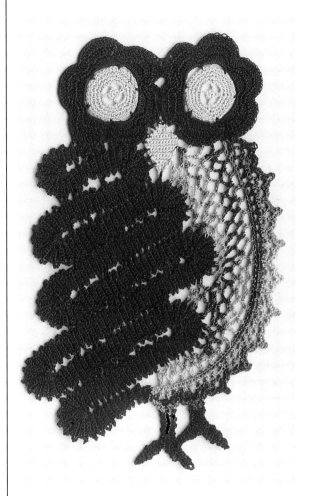

79 The crocheted lace owl

TECHNIQUES
Double crochet (d c), chain (ch), slip stitch (sl st) treble crochet (tr).

ORDER OF WORK
The beak
1 Using beige thread, work the beak, following the chart (Fig. 80). This section is worked in d c. The eyes, wings and breast are all attached to this central section.

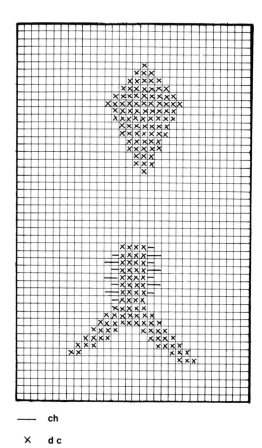

— ch

× d c

80 *The beak and foot of the crocheted lace owl*

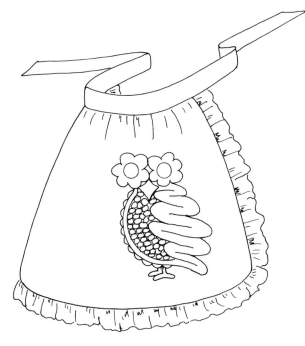

81 *A child's apron*

The first eye

1 Using the beige thread, make a circle with the yarn. Work 8 d c around the circle over both strands. Pull the loose end to draw the circle together.

2 Close the ring with a sl st.

3 *1st row:* 8 ch, miss 1 d c, 1 tr into the next d c (5 ch, miss 1 d c, 1 tr into the next d c). Repeat twice. 5 ch join with a sl st to the 3rd ch of 8 ch.

4 *2nd row:* 6 d c into each space (24 sts).

5 *3rd row:* using d c, increase 1 st in sixth, twelfth, eighteenth and twenty-fourth sts (28 sts).

6 *4th row:* using d c, increase 1 st in seventh, fourteenth, twenty-first and twenty-eighth sts (32 sts).

7 *5th row:* using d c, increase 1 st in eighth, sixteenth, twenty-fourth and thirty-second sts (36 sts).

8 *6th row:* join in the brown thread. 1 d c, (6 ch, miss 5 d c, 1 d c into the next d c). Repeat five times and join with a sl st.

9 Into the spaces work (2 d c, 8 tr, 2 d c). Repeat five times and join with a sl st.

10 *8th row:* (2 d c, 1 tr, increase by working 2 tr into the next 4 tr, increase once in the next st, 1 tr, 2 d c). Repeat five times.

11 *9th row:* 3 ch, 2 tr, 2 tr into the next stitch, 2 tr into the next stitch, 2 tr, 2 tr into the next stitch, 3 tr. Join to the beak on the tenth and eleventh tr of the fifth petal, and the third and fourth tr on the sixth petal on the first eye.

The second eye

1 Work as for the first eye, joining to the petals of the first eye at the fourth and fifth petal, and again to the beak at fifth and sixth petals.

The wings

1 Join the brown threads to the tenth tr of the fourth petal. Work 2 d c, 5 ch, Turn. 2 d c, join to the ninth tr. Turn. 2 d c, 5 ch. Turn.

2 3 d c, join to eighth tr. Turn.

3 3 d c, 5 ch. Turn.

4 4 d c, join to seventh tr. Turn.

5 4 d c, 5 ch. Turn. 5 ch.

44

6 The wings are worked in 5 d c, 5 ch, joining to the respective picot of the previous row.

The breast

1 *1st row*: work 66 ch. Turn.
2 *2nd row*: work 1 d c into each ch. Turn.
3 *3rd row*: work 1 d c, 3 ch, miss 1 d c, 1 d c into the next st. Repeat this along the length. Fasten into petal, wings and tail as it is worked.
4 *4th and 5th rows*: work in 3 ch, 1 d c. Turn.
5 *6th row*: work the edging (3 d c into the first space, 3 d c, 3 ch, 3 d c into the second space. 3 d c into the third space). Repeat 10 times. Cut off the thread and rejoin on the inside of the foundation chain.
6 1 d c, 5 ch, miss 2 ch, 1 d c. Repeat 22 times. Fill in the breast using 1 d c, 5 ch pattern.

The feet

1 Start by crocheting directly on to the breast. Follow the chart, noting the ch sts used to turn each d c row.

4 · CRAKE
torchon lace

USE: guest towel decoration

THREADS: Bouc Linen 100/2 white; gimp thread, Gütermann buttonhole thread, shade No. 230. Fifty-two pairs of bobbins, one single and one pair, *or* two pairs, of gimp threads, depending upon which direction the bird is facing

TECHNIQUES

Cl st, h st, d st, torchon ground, spider, passing a gimp, d st edge, footside with passive threads, tally, fastening off a decorative edge.

ORDER OF WORK

1 Start at the top RH corner. Put up a pin at (a) (Fig. 83). Hang on six open pairs.
2 Take the RH pair, cl st to the left through three pairs. Twist the workers once. Leave two pairs.

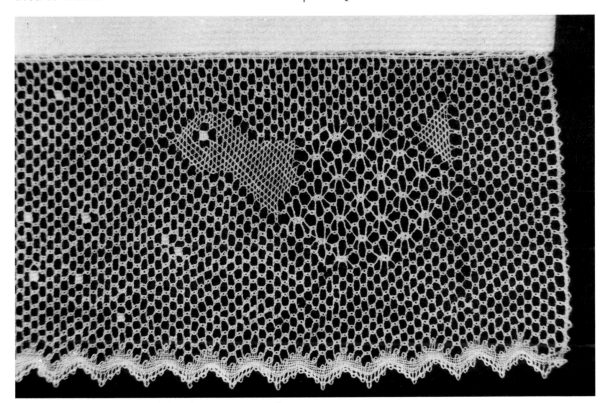

82 The crake, torchon edging for a guest towel

45

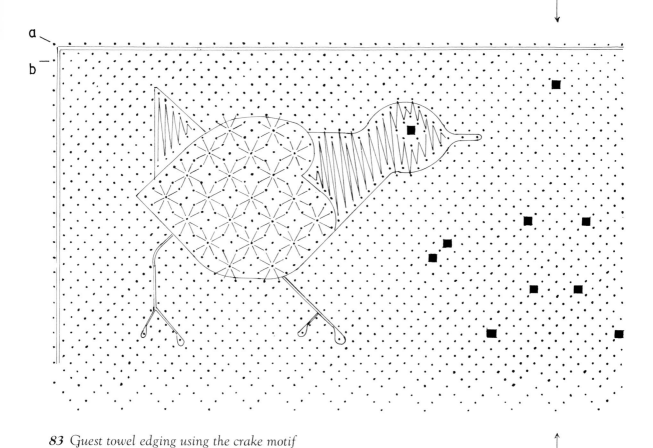

83 Guest towel edging using the crake motif

3 Put up a pin at (b). Hang on two pairs. Twist the RH pair twice.

4 Cl st through the two pairs, twist the workers once.

5 Repeat **3** and **4** until all the pins have been put in, pairs hung on and worked through at the top edge. The remaining pairs will work the cl st zig-zag edge. The two passive (footing) pairs are used within this edge.

6 Start to work the lace from the LH corner, taking in a new pair from the RH side for each diagonal row. The ground is worked in torchon ground (p. 33). The zig-zag edge is worked in cl st, with a d st edge (Fig. 72). Pairs are brought in when working in the RH direction, and then thrown out again when working in the LH direction.

7 The footing is worked using a four-about-the-pin edge (straight edge) (Fig. 3).

8 Hang in the gimp threads as required. The same gimp is used to work the body, neck, head and feet.

9 A separate gimp will be needed for the tail. The neck and tail are worked in h st, a tally for the eye and h st torchon ground for the beak.

10 Cross the gimps (p. 30) between the neck and the body. Spiders are worked in the body section, three twists on each leg.

11 Note the position of the tallies (Fig. 83) and method of working (Fig. 84).

To finish the edging

1 Gradually throw out three pairs in the zig-zag edge. Complete the ground etc., leaving one row of horizontal pinholes unworked.

2 Push down seven or eight rows of pins. Take out the other rows.

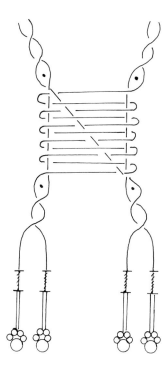

84 A tally

3 Working from the footside, cl st the ground stitch pairs through two pairs of passive threads used in the footing. Twist each pair twice. Put up the pins between these pairs in the row of unworked horizontal pinholes, cross each pair.
4 Turn the pillow round and bring the pairs round each side of the pins. The bobbins are now on top of the lace.
5 Using a pair from the zig-zag edge, work two rows of cl st through all the pairs.
6 Tie and cut off all the threads (Fig. 64).

MOUNTING

1 If necessary, make narrow hems along the two long edges and one short edge, a wider one along the bottom edge.
2 Place the RSs together and using close overcasting sew the two together.
3 From the WS press the seam flat. Take care not to catch the ground with the point of the iron.

5 · CRAKE
Binche lace

USE: the lid of a hand-made box

THREADS: DMC Retors d'Alsace/Broder Machine No. 50, shade Nos 745 (gold), 350 (red) 944 (grey) and black

85 A box lid decorated with the crake motif, worked in Binche lace

TECHNIQUES

Cl st, d st, d st edge braid, simple edge braid, stitch-and-twist braid, ladder, tally, plait-with-picot, leaf plait, changing workers, large snowflake (Binche filling), sewings, tying off several threads, Bruges flower lace leaf.

ORDER OF WORK
The body

1 Along the line at (a) (Fig. 86) put up three pins. Using black thread, hang on six pairs.
2 Work a d st edge braid (Fig. 72) to outline the body. Follow the directional arrows. Note the b sts and the pivoting at the tip of the tail.
3 Following Fig. 87 work the filling. Start at the tip of the tail. The outer line of the snowflake is worked in d st and the centre of the snowflake is worked in cl st.
4 As the filling progresses, pairs are added gradually, used, and then sewn into the edge. They are used again to work the filling.

Finally, sew out, firm the threads, tie each
pair in a reef knot and cut off the threads.

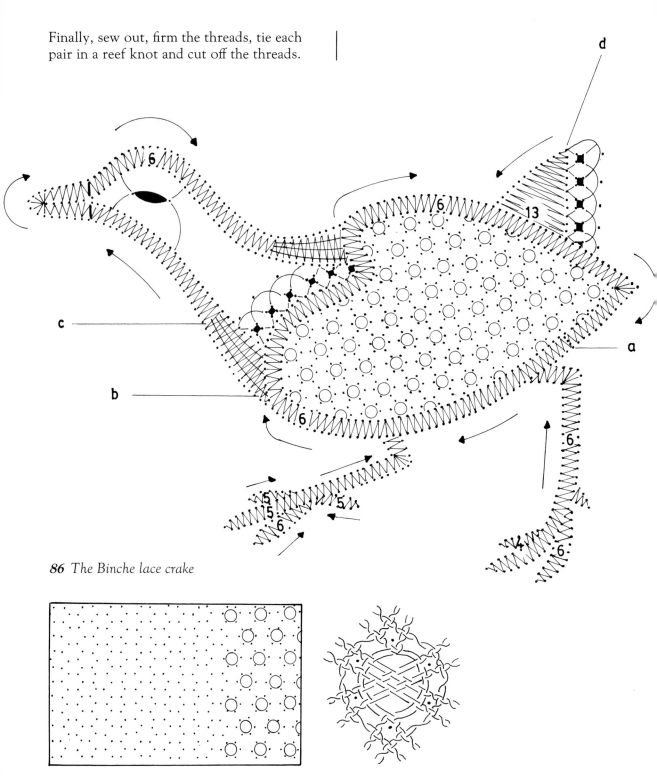

86 *The Binche lace crake*

87 *The large snowflake, Binche filling*

The head

1 At (b), using red threads, sew in three pairs, one passive pair and two edge pairs at the RH edge.

2 Work a d st edge, stitch-and-twist braid, gradually hanging in four more pairs. Follow the worker line carefully, sewing the worker into the pinloop edge of the body when necessary.

3 At (c), a d st edge braid is worked. Upon reaching the thicker line marked for the beak, introduce a gold worker pair, by working the edge stitch and one pair of passive threads. Lay the worker pair to the back of the work, and lay in the new worker pair. Continue working. These pairs are later tied and cut off.

4 Finish working the beak and change the workers to red again. Complete the head and neck as indicated on the pricking.

5 Work the eye (using black thread) by sewing in the four pairs for the two plaits. When completed use the outside pairs of each plait to work the leaf plait. The two inside pairs are carried over the top of the leaf plait and used again to work the two plaits, which are then sewn out, tied and cut off.

6 Using red threads, work the tally and plait-with-picot edging at the base of the neck.

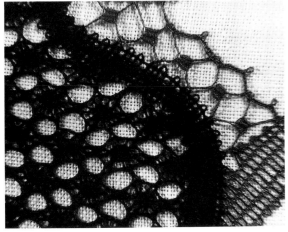

88 Detail of the edging used on the neck of the crake

The tail

1 At (d) put up a pin. Set up the tail as for a

89 Detail of the tail

Bruges flower lace leaf (Fig. 68), using red thread.

2 Increase the pairs to 13, using a ladder to decorate the tail.

3 Sew out into the pinloop edge of the body braid. Tie and cut off the threads.

4 Work the tally and plait-with-picot edging to decorate the tail.

The legs

1 Work the centre claw and leg first, using a simple edge braid. Use five pairs of grey thread and one pair of black thread to outline the leg at the RH edge. Sew out into the pinloop edge of the braid.

2 Work the other small claws in the same manner, sewing out into the pinloop edge of the leg braid.

6 · CRAKE
Irish lace

USE: boudoir cushion

THREADS AND MATERIALS: DMC
Retors d'Alsace/Broder Machine Nos 30 and
50, DMC Coton Perlé No. 12, organdie,
coarse tulle, cover cloth, architect's paper,
and ballpoint needles

90 *The crake worked in Irish lace (detail)*

TECHNIQUES
Couching, seeds/pops, Irish lace filling Nos 1,
2 and 4.

PREPARATION
Prepare the organdie and tulle as described
for the Irish lace bee (p. 12).

ORDER OF WORK
1 Couch the design lines of the head, neck,
legs, small wing and tail (Fig. 92).
2 Cut away the organdie around the couched
areas. Observing Fig. 90 couch along the
wing and body lines.
3 Work Irish lace filling No. 2 (Fig. 93) in
section 1, Irish lace filling No. 4 (Fig. 94) in
section 2, and Irish lace filling No. 1 (Fig. 18)
in the beak, section 3 using the thicker
Retors d'Alsace thread.

COMPLETION
Finish off the work as described for the Irish
lace bee (p. 14).

91 *A boudoir cushion*

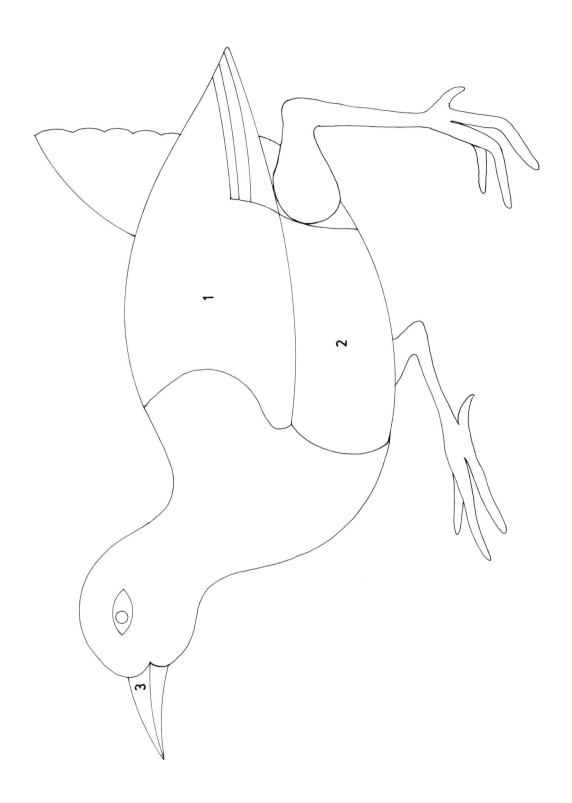

92 The crake motif

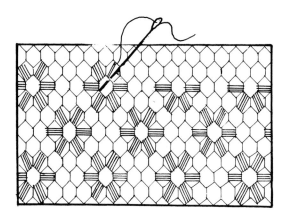

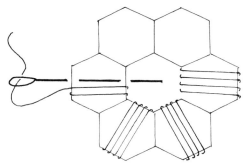

93 *Irish lace filling No. 2*

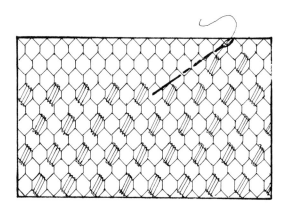

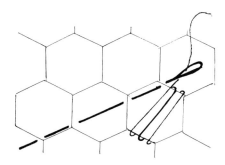

94 *Irish lace filling No. 4*

7 · PUFFIN
torchon lace

USE: guest towel decoration

THREADS: Swedish linen Bocken 100/2 in white, Gütermann buttonhole thread, shade No. 230, for the gimp. Fifty-two pairs of bobbins, three gimps

95 *The Norwegian puffin, torchon edging for a guest towel (detail)*

TECHNIQUES
Cl st, h st, d st, h st ground, torchon ground, crossing a gimp, d st edge, footside with two passives, tally, roseground, tying off several threads.

ORDER OF WORK
1 Set up the pricking as described for working the torchon crake (p. 45).
2 Work as much as possible of the main ground, torchon ground (p. 33), round the shape of the puffin.
3 Pass the gimp through the appropriate pairs (p. 30), and work the beak in cl st.
4 When (a) (Fig. 96a) is reached, work the torchon ground stitches into the neck and side of the head.
5 Add the second gimp thread at the top of the cheek. The two gimps must lie close together.

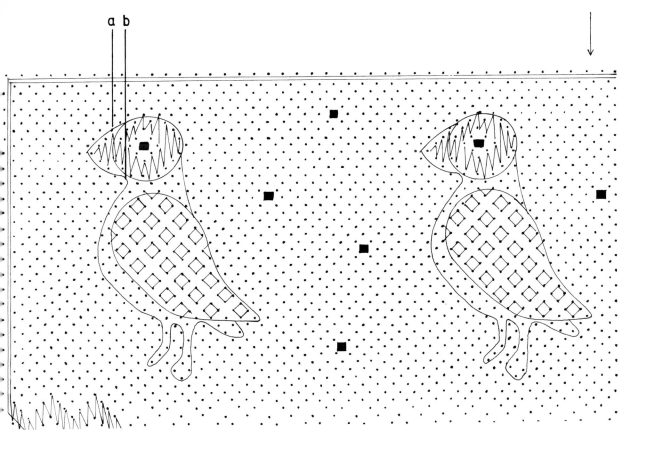

96 *The puffins worked in torchon lace*

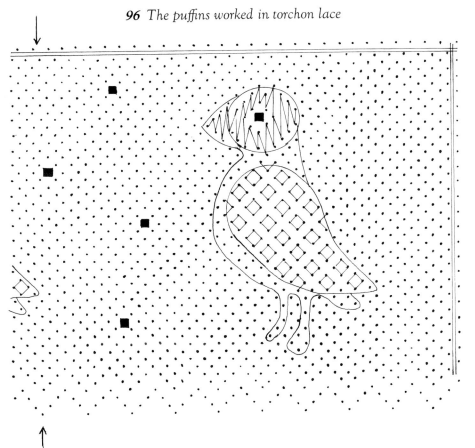

6 Work the eye in h st with a central tally, moving the gimp threads and working the torchon ground stitch.

7 At (b) the first gimp passes round the neck, breast and down to work the feet and tail.

8 Work more of the torchon ground in the chest and neck. The third gimp thread is added at the top of the wing.

9 Some of the roseground (Fig. 97) must be worked in the wing before the h st ground in the head can be completed.

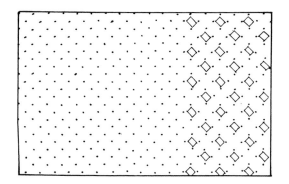

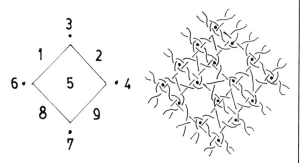

97 Roseground variation

10 The second gimp continues round the neck and is worked out together with the third gimp at the top of the wing.

11 Complete all the ground, footing and zig-zag edge until one row of unworked horizontal pinholes remain. Work this last row of pinholes as described for the torchon crake (p. 46).

MOUNTING
This edging is mounted in a similar way to the torchon crake guest towel (p. 47).

8 · PUFFIN
Valenciennes lace

USE: a picture

THREAD: Bouc cotton No. 100

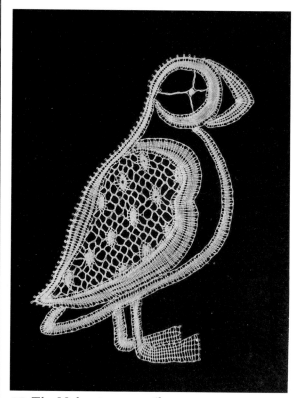

98 The Valenciennes puffin

TECHNIQUES
Cl st, ladder, straight edge (four-about-the-pin edge) braid, picot, plait, sewings, tying off several threads, connecting two plaits (Valenciennes lace), snowflakes (two methods).

ORDER OF WORK
1 At (a) (Fig. 99) put up a pin. Hang on five open pairs.

2 Following the worker line and working a cl st four-about-the-pin edge braid, work the head.

3 Gradually increase to 12 pairs as marked on the pricking.

4 As the braid narrows, gradually throw out four pairs.

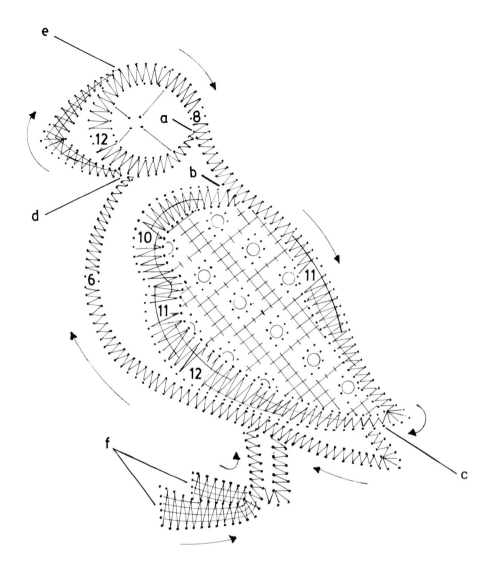

99 *The Valenciennes lace puffin, the design based upon a Norwegian stamp*

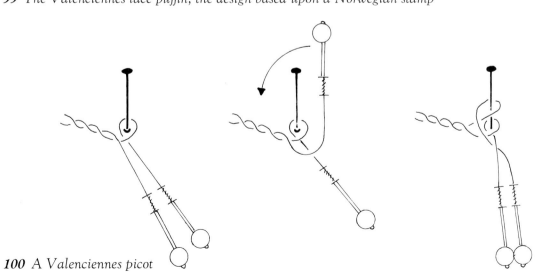

100 A Valenciennes picot

5 Work picots (Fig. 100) at the outer edge. Complete this section by introducing ladders as marked. Throw out and hang in pairs, working the ladders in the wider section of the braid around the wing.

6 Sew out at (b) the few remaining pairs. Tie and cut off.

7 Along the edge at (c) sew in seven pairs. Using the same braid as before, work this section, decreasing to six pairs as indicated. Sew out, etc., at (d).

8 At (e) start to work the beak. Sew in five pairs. Work the first two rows in cl st, with a d st edge. From the back of the work hang in two more pairs (seven pairs are now on the pillow).

9 When the seventh pin has been worked hang in one more pair.

10 The next row will now work as follows: cl st through two pairs, twist the workers, cl st through one passive pair, twist the workers, cl st through two passive pairs, work the edge stitch. The twists form the ladders.

11 Reduce the pairs to four, sew out, etc., close to (d).

The feet and legs

1 Set up the feet at (f), working a straight edge and a stitch-and-twist filling in the feet.

2 The legs are worked in cl st, with a four-about-the-pin edge braid.

The eye

1 The eye is worked by using two plaits, a tally worked with two centre pairs, whilst outer pairs are twisted and used at base of tally to make last two plaits. Each plait is finally sewn out into the braid.

The body filling

1 Study the Valenciennes filling (Figs 101 and 102) very carefully, noting the following:
(a) plaits form the ground, each plait being the same length. Plaits are joined with a cl st using the two centre pairs.
(b) normally pins are not used to support the junction of the plaits. However, Lille pins may be used until you are confident enough to work without them.

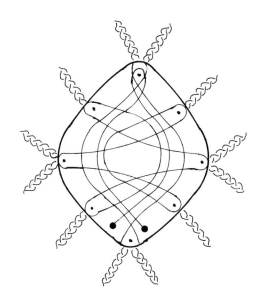

101 Snowflake with a hole

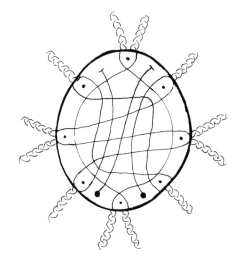

102 Snowflake without a hole

(c) the top LH area of the wing is worked with snowflakes with a small hole (Fig. 101). The snowflakes in the lower RH area are worked without the hole (Fig. 102).

2 The outer line is worked in a d st, the centre being worked in cl st.

3 Great care should be taken when sewing in and sewing out pairs. These techniques, badly worked, will misshape the filling.

9 · PUFFIN
Irish lace

USE: a tray

THREADS AND MATERIALS: DMC
Retors d'Alsace/Broder Machine Nos 30 and
50, DMC Coton Perlé No. 12, organdie,
coarse tulle, cover cloth, architect's paper
and ballpoint needles

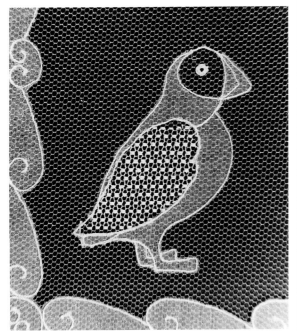

103 The Norwegian puffin worked in Irish lace

TECHNIQUES
Couching, seeds/pops, Irish lace filling No. 3.

PREPARATION
Prepare the organdie and tulle as described
for the Irish lace bee (p. 12).

ORDER OF WORK
1 Couch the 'waves' line, the outer edge and
all the lines of the puffin.
2 Remove the tacking threads and cut away
the organdie from the edge of the 'waves',
the edge of the puffin and inside the head and
wing.
3 Work the seeds/pops (Fig. 44) at the top
corner and in the eyes, Irish lace filling No. 3

in the wings and the twirling (Fig. 46) at the
outer edge, using the thicker Retors
d'Alsace/Broder Machine thread.
4 Do not cut away the organdie and tulle
under the twirling.

104 Puffin motif worked in Irish lace (variation)

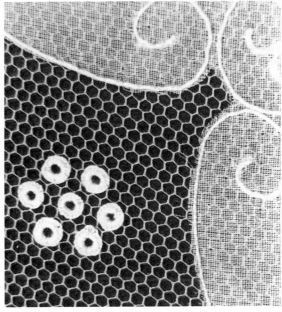

*105 The top right-hand corner of the tray
showing the seeds/pops*

COMPLETION
Finish off the work as described for the Irish lace bee (p. 14). The lace should be mounted by a specialist picture framer, who will be able to seal the edge of the glass to the frame. This will ensure that fluids do not penetrate through to the lace.

106 A tray cloth, a variation of the Irish lace puffin

10 · PUFFIN
crocheted lace

USE: a wallhanging

THREADS AND EQUIPMENT: four large wooden beads, a pair of No. 3 (6½ mm) knitting needles, crochet cotton DMC Cordonnet Special 40, No. 2.00 mm crochet hook

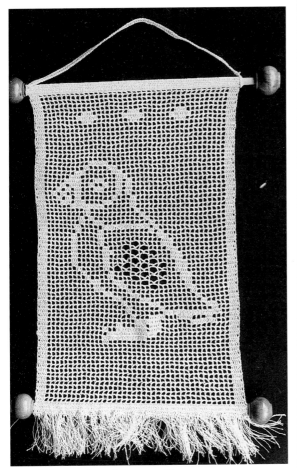

107 The crocheted lace puffin

TECHNIQUES
Treble crochet (tr), chain (ch).

ORDER OF WORK
1 Work 132 ch, and 3 ch to turn.
2 Work 1 tr into each ch.
3 Repeat 2, five times more.
4 The ground is worked in 1 tr, 3 ch.
5 Each 'dot' on the chart represents a cluster of tr, 4 tr in a single one, 7 tr in two, 10 tr in three clusters, etc.
6 The centre decoration is worked in ch st.
7 Carefully follow the chart and completely crochet the design.

MOUNTING
1 Cut the knitting needles the width of the lace plus the depth of the wooden bead. File away any rough edges. Polish, paint or stain the beads and leave to dry thoroughly.
2 Turn over the upper and lower edges of the lace on to the WS. Hem firmly.
3 Crochet the hanging cord. Slide the knitting needle through the loop of the cord and the top of the lace and the other loop of the cord.
4 Use a clear glue to attach the wooden beads to each end of the knitting needle. Mount the bottom edge in a similar way.
5 Prepare the fringe. This is made by winding the crochet cotton around a box, so as to give a 10 cm fringe. Cut the thread, fold in half, and attach the looped threads to the crocheted edge as you would when sewing in a thread into the edge of a braid.

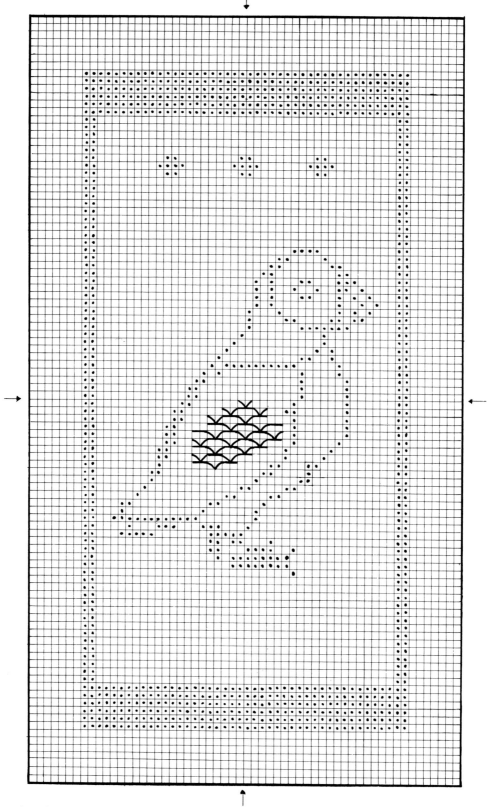

108 A crocheted wall hanging using the
puffin motif

60

11 · MOTMOT
Binche lace

USE: a picture

THREADS: DMC Retors d'Alsace/Broder Machine No. 50, shade Nos 206 (green), 944 (grey), 744 (yellow), 798 (blue) and a selection of brown and cream threads

109 *The Binche lace motmot*

TECHNIQUES
D st edge braid (cl st and h st), sewing out and tying off several pairs, a tally, simple snowflake, large snowflake (h st), small snowflake, simple braid, leaf plaits.

ORDER OF WORK
1 Along a line at (a) (Fig. 111) put up five pins. Hang on five pairs wound in green thread, and one pair in grey thread, the worker pair.

2 Following the worker lines, start by working the beak from left to right. The braid has a d st edge on the outer edge, and a simple edge at the inner edge. The braid itself is worked in cl st. Note the b sts, and the directional lines.

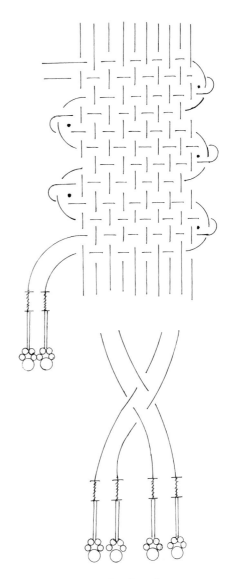

110 *A simple edge, cl st braid*

3 At (b) sew in one pair of green threads at the LH edge. Change to yellow workers after working the edge stitch and one pair of passive threads. Work this section in a cl st, d st edge braid.

4 At (c) change to green workers and add one more green pair. Work this section, first

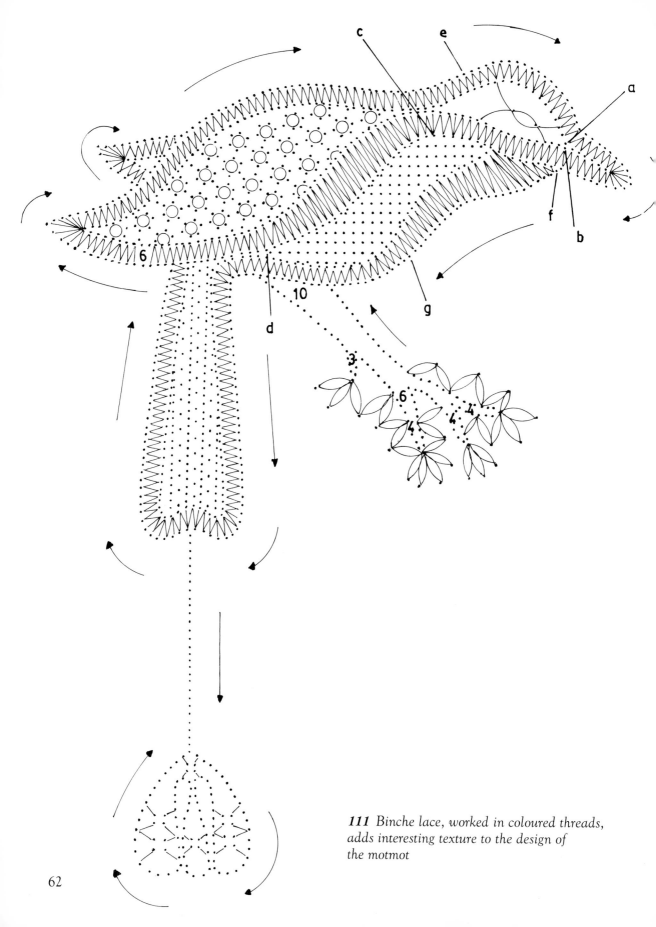

111 Binche lace, worked in coloured threads, adds interesting texture to the design of the motmot

in h st and then in cl st, following Fig. 109. Throw out one pair (Fig. 112) (six pairs on the pillow).

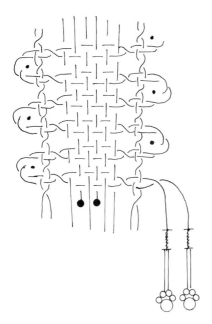

112 Throwing out a pair

5 Work the cl st braid, pivoting around the pin at the base of the tail (b st) to (e), where the worker pair is exchanged for a blue worker. Finish working the braid and join the braid to the setting up pins, etc.
6 Using the blue thread, work a leaf plait for the eye (Fig. 75).
7 At (f) sew in a green pair and a yellow pair. Sew in three green passive pairs and one green edge pair. Carefully follow the worker line, twisting the passive pair only after each cl st in the d st edge braid.
8 Continue using this braid, changing to a cl st braid at (g). Throw out a green centre pair as the braid narrows.
9 The worker is changed to red, to work 4 cm of braid and again, to green, to work the last section of the tail.
10 Sew out the threads into the pinloops and bar of the braid.
11 Work the small length of second wing braid, using a four-about-the-pin braid and green thread.
12 Work the fillings.

The wing (the large snowflake [Fig. 87])
1 Observe Fig. 111 and note the following:
(a) using the green thread, sew in the pairs at the neck and work in a horizontal line if you find it easier.
(b) the outer ring is worked in d st and the centre in h st. Follow Fig. 111 very carefully. Fine pins (Lille pins) may be used to support the plaits if necessary.

The tail (the simple snowflake [Fig. 113])
1 Using green thread, work the simple snowflakes. Make two twists on each pair of diagonal bobbins. The centre is worked in cl st.

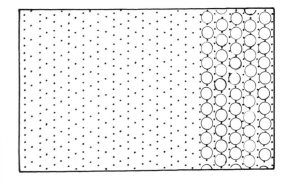

113 A simple snowflake, Binche lace

The chest (the small snowflake [Fig. 114])
1 Use yellow thread, setting up at the throat. The filling may be worked in a horizontal direction if you find it easier.

The branch
1 Use a mixture of browns and cream thread. Observe Figs 109 and 111. A simple edge braid is used, requiring four to six pairs in the narrow areas, and ten pairs in the wider areas.

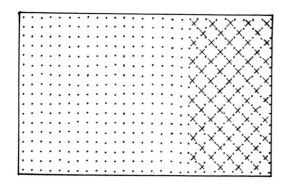

114 *A small snowflake, Binche lace*

The leaves and flowers

Work the leaves first, using leaf plaits (Fig. 75). Use two different coloured pairs in each plait. When the workers are changed a different coloured leaf will result. The flower plaits are worked using shades of pink when the leaves have been completed.

12 · MOTMOT
Irish lace

USE: a mobile

THREADS AND MATERIALS: DMC Retors d'Alsace/Broder Machine Nos 30 and 50, DMC Coton Perlé No. 12, organdie, coarse tulle, cover cloth, architect's paper, a ballpoint needle, mobile frame (36 × 30 cm)

115 *The Irish lace motmot (see jacket)*

TECHNIQUES

Couching, seeds/pops, twirling, Irish lace filling Nos 1, 2 and 3.

PREPARATION

Prepare the organdie and tulle as described for the Irish lace bee (p. 12).

ORDER OF WORK

1 Place a piece of organdie, the length and width of the entire branch, in place. Tack close to the design.
2 Using the finer thread in the needle, couch the Coton Perlé thread along the line of the branches and foot.

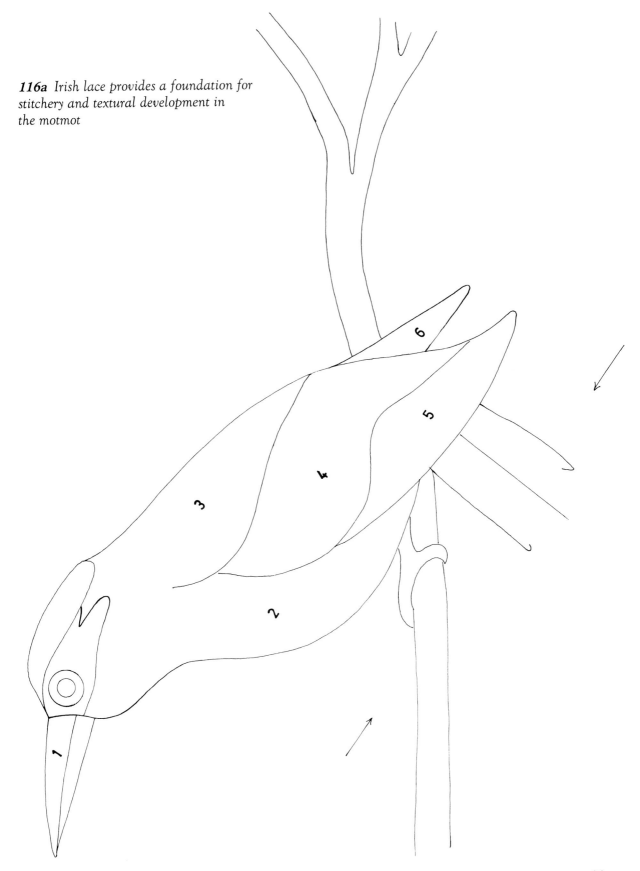

116a Irish lace provides a foundation for stitchery and textural development in the motmot

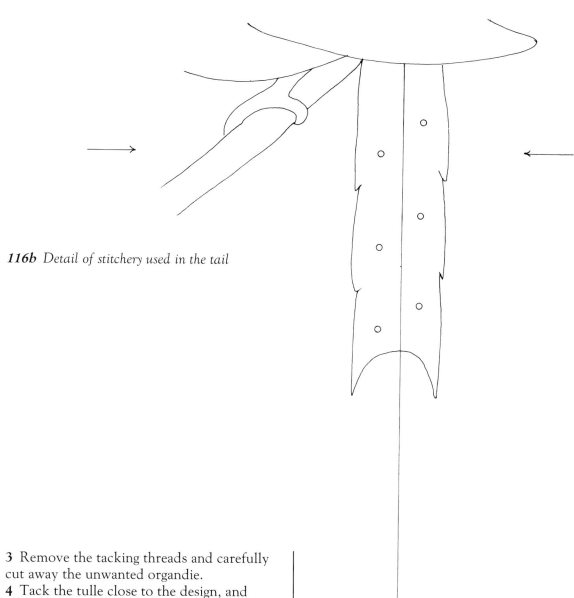

116b Detail of stitchery used in the tail

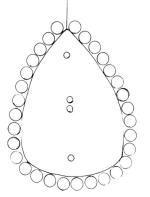

3 Remove the tacking threads and carefully cut away the unwanted organdie.

4 Tack the tulle close to the design, and couch the remaining design lines. Using the thicker Retors d'Alsace/Broder Machine, work Irish lace filling No. 2 (Fig. 93) in section 2, filling No. 1 (Fig. 18) in sections 1, 3, 5 and 6, and filling No. 3 (Fig. 43) in section 4.

5 Work the eye, using one flower of section 2. Seeds/pops (Fig. 44) are used to work the tail, and twirling (Fig. 46) decorates the edge of the lower section of the tail.

COMPLETION

Finish off the work as described for the Irish lace bee (p. 14).

1 The Royal Mail stamp of a bee

2 The Royal Mail stamp of a dragonfly

3 The Royal Mail stamp of a ladybird

4 The Belgian stamp of an owl

5 The Rwandan stamp of a crake

6 The Norwegian stamp of a puffin

7 *The Nicaraguan stamp of a motmot*

8 *The French stamp of a cockerel*

9 *The Hong Kong stamp of a butterfly*

10 *The Hungarian stamp of a butterfly*

11 *The Hungarian stamp of a moth*

12 *The Antiguan stamp of a butterfly*

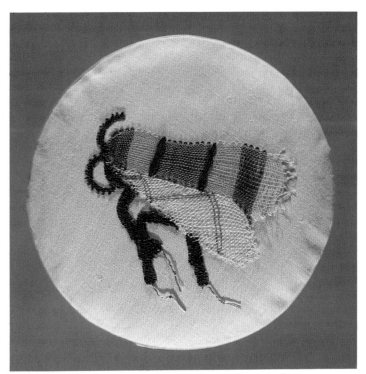

13 The bee, simple in shape, using traditional colours

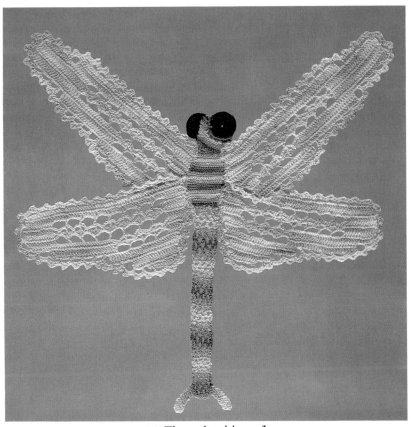

14 The crocheted dragonfly

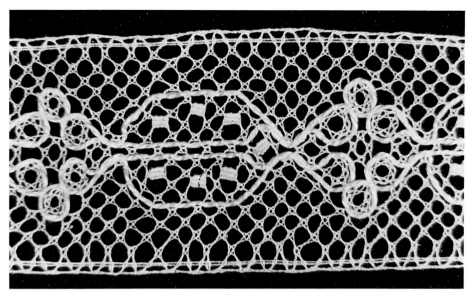

15 A ladybird motif, worked in torchon lace

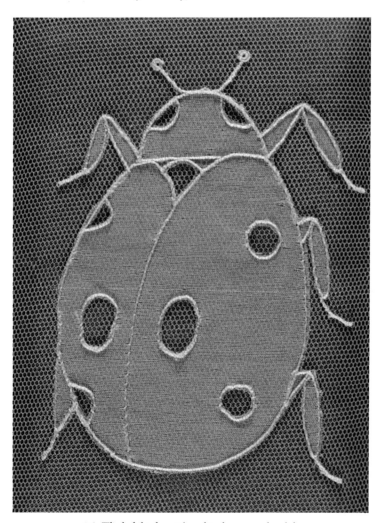

16 The ladybird motif used to decorate a box lid

17 *The Bruges flower lace owl*

18 *The crocheted Belgian owl*

19 *The crake motif worked in Binche lace*

20 Details of the branch and flowers for the Binche lace motmot (see Fig. 109)

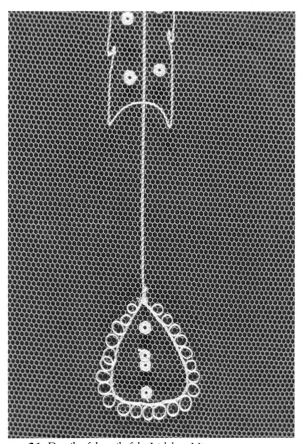

21 Details of the tail of the Irish lace Nicaraguan motmot (see Fig. 115)

22 The French cockerel motif worked in Bruges flower lace

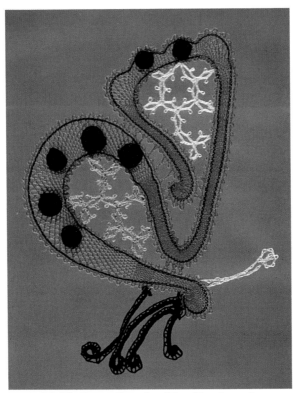

23 The Bruges flower lace Hong Kong butterfly

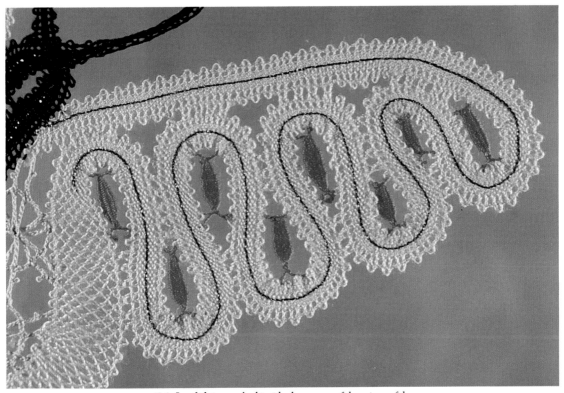

24 Leaf plaits worked inside the curves of the wings of the
Hungarian Russian tape lace butterfly (see Fig. 186)

25 The Antiguan butterfly worked in Duchesse lace

26 The wine bottle apron

13 · MOTMOT
needle lace

USE: a picture

THREADS: DMC Special Dentelles, DMC
Retors d'Alsace/Broder Machine No. 50

117 The needle lace motmot

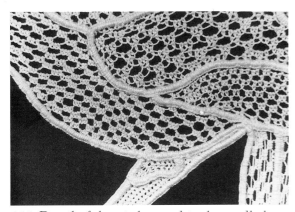

*118 Detail of the stitches used in the needle lace
motmot*

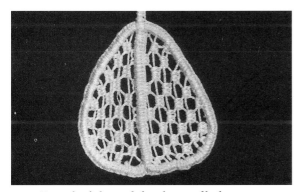

119 Detail of the tail for the needle lace motmot

TECHNIQUES
Cordonnet, cordonnette, couronne, single
Brussels, double Brussels, treble Brussels,
corded single Brussels, corded treble
Brussels, pea stitch, pea stitch variation.

PREPARATION
Prepare as for the needle lace bee (p. 15).

ORDER OF WORK
1 Plan out the laying of the cordonnet well
in advance. Use two threads of the Special
Dentelles and the finer thread in the needle
to lay the cordonnet, remembering to keep
the couching stitches 2 mm apart. It may be
necessary to split the threads in some places
and retrace the line with the same thread to
give a two-line thickness.

2 The fillings are marked numerically:
(1) single Brussels (Fig. 25);
(2) double Brussels (Fig. 120);
(3) treble Brussels (Fig. 122);
(4) corded single Brussels (Fig. 27);
(5) corded treble Brussels (Fig. 26);
(6) pea stitch (Fig. 24);
(7) pea stitch variation (Fig. 28);
(8) a couronne (Fig. 123).

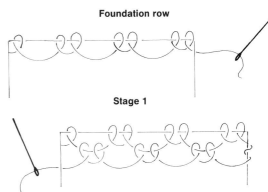

Foundation row

Stage 1

120 Double Brussels filling

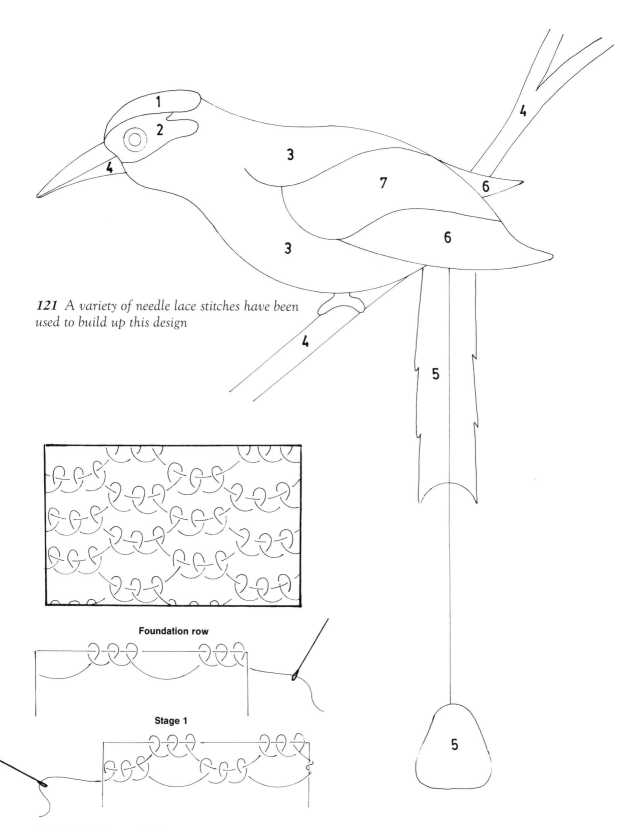

121 A variety of needle lace stitches have been used to build up this design

Foundation row

Stage 1

122 Treble Brussels filling

14 · COCKEREL
Bruges flower lace

USE: a picture

THREADS: Gütermann machine thread, shade Nos 155, 285, 288, 414, 837, 869, 925, 929, 979

124 The Bruges flower lace cockerel

TECHNIQUES
Cl st, d st, h st, d st edge braid, ladder, h st filling braid, finishing a braid, honeycomb filling, sewings, tying off several threads, hanging in and throwing out pairs.

ORDER OF WORK
1 At (a) (Fig. 125), using shade No. 288, set up as for a leaf (Fig. 68), on the first three pins only (six pairs). Work in a h st, d st edge braid. Hang in more pairs (Fig. 126), until there are nine pairs on the pillow. Reduce to eight pairs above the junction with the top feathers.
2 Change to cl st, finishing with a scroll (Fig. 127).

123 Working a couronne

COMPLETION
Follow instructions **4** to **7** inclusive for the needle lace bee (p. 19) to work the cordonnette (Fig. 30), using six strands of Special Dentelles.

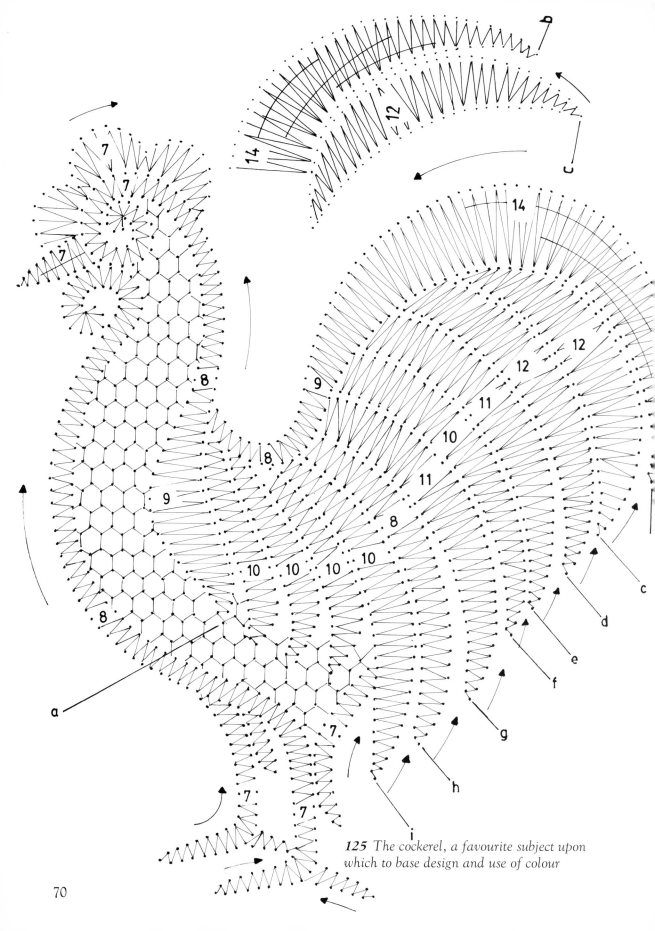

125 The cockerel, a favourite subject upon which to base design and use of colour

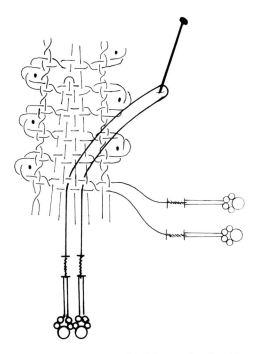

126 *Hanging in a pair of bobbins, cl st braid*

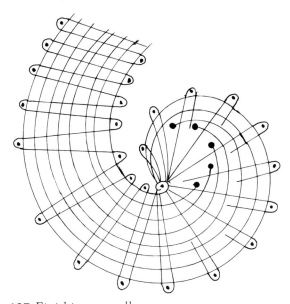

127 *Finishing a scroll*

3 At (b), and using shade No. 288, set up as for a leaf (Fig. 68) on the first three pins only. Using a cl st, d st edge braid, work the feather. Ladders are used as marked. Other coloured threads may be introduced, gradually increasing to 14 pairs.

4 As the braid progresses, reduce the passive threads to nine and then eight as indicated.

Sew out the remaining threads into the pinloops and bars of the first braid.

5 Each feather has the edge pair worked in the main colour of the previous feather.

6 Feathers (c) to (i) are set up, worked and sewn out in the same way. The passive threads are divided to work the feathers, half in cl st and half in h st. Sewings join the feathers.

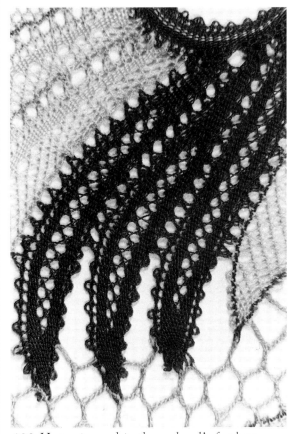

128 *H st vein used in the cockerel's feathers*

7 The number of pairs required to work each feather is marked on Fig. 125. The three small centre feathers are worked in shade No. 288, with a h st vein.

8 Work the chest braid, cl st, d st edge braid, in shade No. 285. Note the directional arrows, starting at the claw and finishing with a scroll at the neck (Fig. 127).

9 Work the other leg and the small claws, noting the number of pairs required as marked on Fig. 125.

10 Work the beak, using shade No. 414, by setting up as for a Bruges flower lace leaf (six pairs) (Fig. 68). A ladder divides the upper and lower beak. Sew out into the braid, tie off, etc.

11 The cockscomb, shade 155, is set up by sewing seven pairs into the edge of the beak (Fig. 129). This section is worked in the same manner as a Bruges flower lace flower. It is worked in h st, throwing out pairs as it finally narrows. Sew out and tie off the four pairs.

12 Using shade No. 285, work the honeycomb filling (Fig. 130), using plaits and false plaits (Fig. 67).

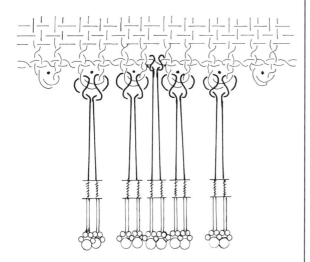

129 Sewing in several pairs of bobbins

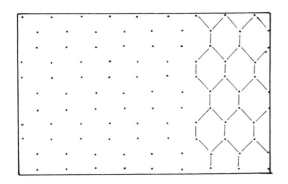

130 Honeycomb filling, Bruges flower lace

15 · COCKEREL
Duchesse lace

USE: a picture

THREADS: Egyptian Cotton No. 60, DMC Coton Perlé No. 12

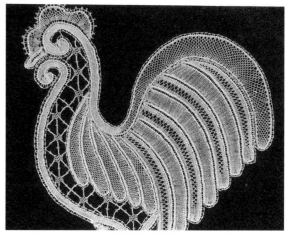

131 The Duchesse lace cockerel (detail)

TECHNIQUES
Cl st, h st, straight edge (four-about-the-pin edge) braid, h st vein, Bruges rib for raised edge, plait-with-picot, h st bud, ladder, sewings, picots.

ORDER OF WORK
1 At (a) in Fig. 132 set up for a curved edge (Fig. 33). Note that a double pair of contour threads are placed in as the braid is set up. This braid is worked in h st.

2 Gradually hang in more pairs until there are 15 pairs on the pillow.

3 Throw out pairs (Fig. 133) as the braid narrows, and when the junction of the last five feathers is reached work the braid in cl st. This section is finished with a scroll (Fig. 134), at the eye. Note the false plait (Fig. 67) joining the scroll to the braid.

4 At (b) set up a curved edge (Fig. 33), again using a double contour pair (one thick and one thin pair). Look at Fig. 132 and you will see that eight pairs are used.

5 Work this braid in cl st, finishing with a scroll (Fig. 134).

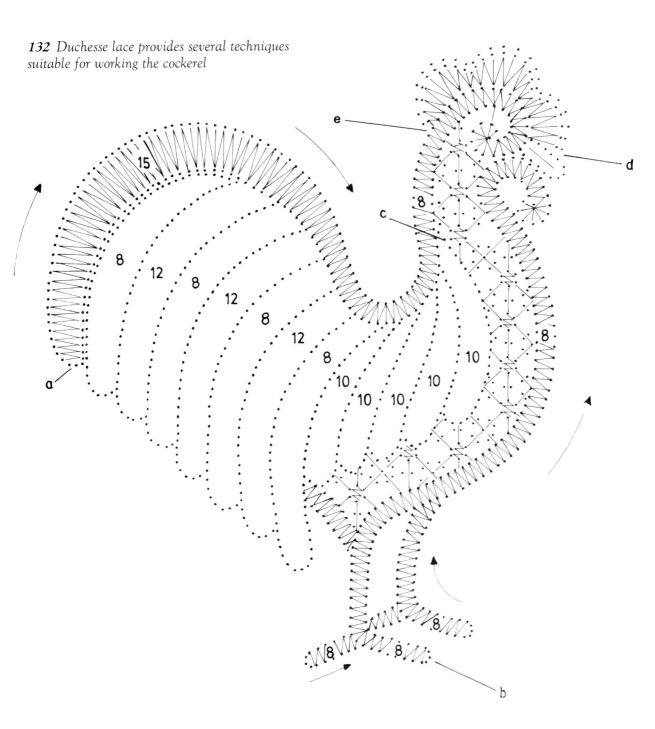

132 Duchesse lace provides several techniques suitable for working the cockerel

6 At (c) sew in five pairs for working the Bruges rib and hang in the contour pair (one thick and one thin thread). Work and turn the rib (Fig. 11). Work the feather in h st, with a straight edge.

7 Sew out into the first braid. Select seven pairs (new threads may be added if necessary) and make a group with these threads.

Following Fig. 132 sew the group of threads to the edge of the feather using the seventh pair of threads to do so. Keep the threads in order and do not let them cross.

8 Work the short length to the top of the next feather in Bruges rib, turn, and work down the feather in h st, sewing under both bars and over the group of straight threads.

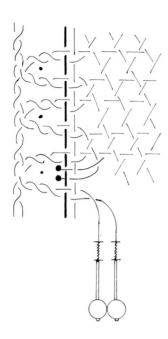

133 Throwing out a pair, Duchesse lace

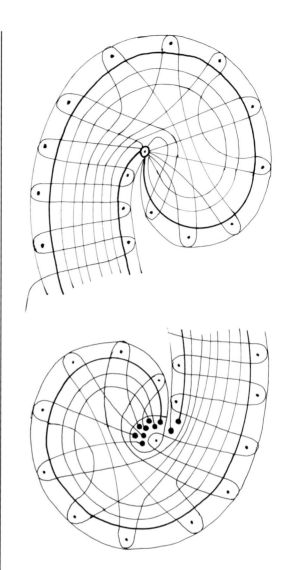

134 Working a Duchesse scroll

9 Work the next three feathers in the same
way. The other seven feathers are basically
worked in the same manner, but they are
worked alternately in cl st with a h st vein,
and cl st only.

10 Work the other leg, setting up as for a
curved edge. Complete the feet and the small
length of braid under the tail feathers.

11 The beak is worked in a similar manner
to the feet. This time a ladder separates the
upper and lower beaks.

12 At (d) sew in six pairs and hang in a
contour pair. The cockscomb is worked in
the following order:

(a) the first section is worked half in cl st and
half in h st;

(b) the second section is worked all in h st;

(c) the third section is worked half in h st and
half in cl st, throwing out pairs as the braid
narrows.

13 Sew out the last three pairs into the edge
of the braid at (e). Tie and cut off.

14 Work the filling of h st buds and plait-
with-picot (Fig. 136).

*135 Details of the Duchesse lace cockerel, the
filling, raised work and the feathers*

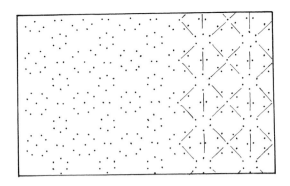

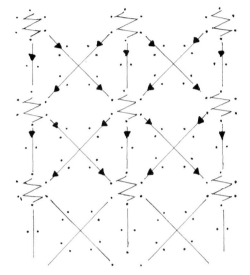

136 Plait-with-picot/h st bud filling

16 · COCKEREL
Irish lace

USE: a mobile

THREADS AND MATERIALS: DMC Retors d'Alsace/Broder Machine Nos 30 and 50, DMC Coton Perlé No. 12, cover cloth, organdie, coarse tulle, architect's paper, ballpoint needles

137 The cockerel, worked in Irish lace, showing details of the filling

TECHNIQUES
Couching, twirling, Irish lace filling No. 2.

PREPARATION
Prepare the organdie and tulle as described for the Irish lace bee (p. 12).

ORDER OF WORK
1 Observing Fig. 138 couch the Coton Perlé

138 *The cockerel motif worked in Irish lace*

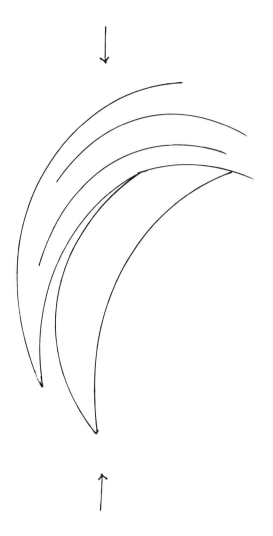

138a The cockerel's tail

threads along the design lines, feathers, head, legs and breast.

2 Cut away the unwanted organdie only, observing Fig. 137.

3 Work Irish lace filling No. 2 (Fig. 93) in the breast, using the thicker Retors d'Alsace. Work the twirling (Fig. 46) at the edge of the cockscomb using the Coton Perlé and the finer Retors d'Alsace/Broder Machine threads.

COMPLETION

Finish off the work as described for the Irish lace bee (p. 14). For mounting as a mobile see Hungarian Moth (p. 109).

17 · COCKEREL
Brussels tape lace

USE: skirt decoration

THREADS AND TAPE: DMC Brillante d'Alsace/Broder Machine 50 (to catch the edges), DMC Special Dentelles (for working the stitches), 3 m narrow Brussels lace tape

NB Photograph overleaf

TECHNIQUES
Russian stitch (herringbone), single wheel, wheel stitch, interwoven Russian stitch, twisted Russian stitch, single Brussels stitch, double Brussels stitch, cluster insertion, branch insertion with wheels.

PREPARATION
Press the tape and prepare the design, etc. as described for the Brussels tape lace dragonfly (p. 21). Check that all the stitching where the tapes have crossed, etc. has been completed before working the Brussels tape lace stitches.

ORDER OF WORK
1 Study Fig. 140 and the fillings used to work this design. The fillings are marked numerically for identification:
(1) wheel stitch (Fig. 141);
(2) Russian stitch (Fig. 142);
(3) Russian stitch, each side of laid middle thread (Fig. 39);
(4) interwoven Russian stitch (Fig. 143);
(5) twisted Russian stitch (Fig. 40);
(6) single Brussels stitch (Fig. 25);
(7) double Brussels stitch (Fig. 120);
(8) cluster insertion (Fig. 144);
(9) branch insertion with wheels (Fig. 145).
2 Carefully remove all the tacking stitches. Press the piece of lace, RS down, and protect the lace with a damp linen cloth.

MOUNTING
Carefully hem the motif(s) in place at the lower edge of the skirt. The lace will maintain its good shape and appearance if the skirt is dry-cleaned rather than washed.

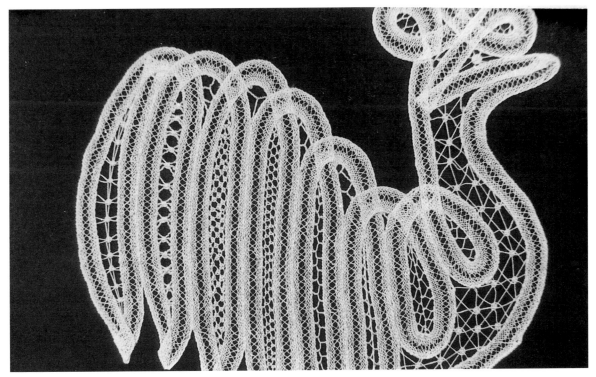

140 The Brussels tape lace cockerel showing a variety of stitches (detail)

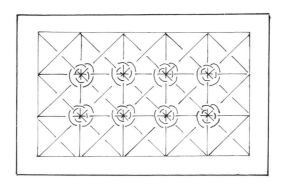

Foundation threads　　　　　　　　　　**Laying final thread while working spider**

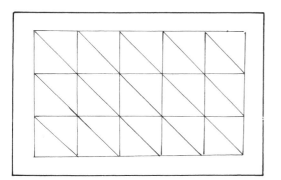　　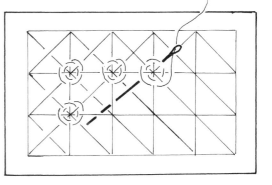

141 Wheel stitch

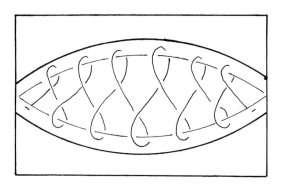

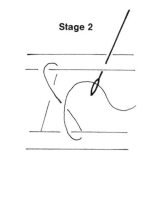

Stage 1

Stage 2

142 *Russian stitch*

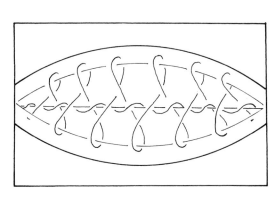

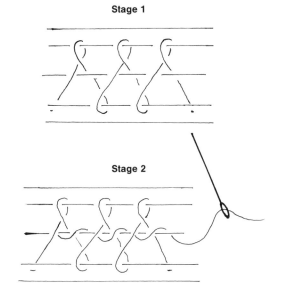

Stage 1

Stage 2

143 *Interwoven Russian stitch*

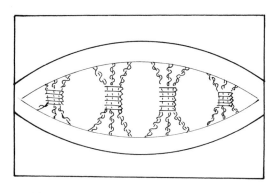

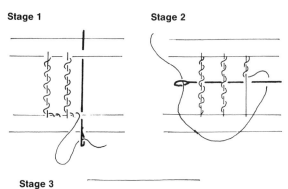

Stage 1

Stage 2

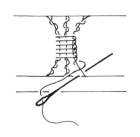

Stage 3

144 *Cluster insertion*

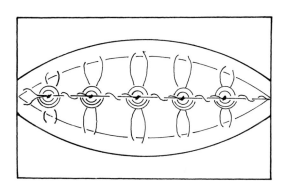

Stage 1

Stage 2

Stage 3

Stage 4

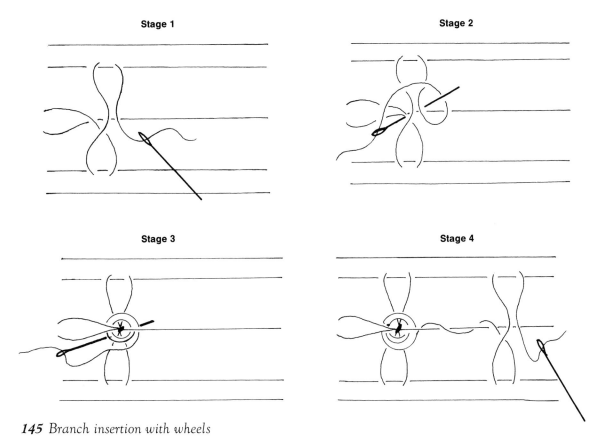

145 Branch insertion with wheels

BUTTERFLIES AND MOTHS

You will find the mobile and placemat themes are continued in this chapter. Several pieces of three-dimensional work will be introduced. The butterflies are worked in a variety of laces to provide a choice for the experienced and inexperienced lacemaker.

The prickings are worked in a traditional manner and an embroidery thread has been introduced to work one of the large butterflies. This thread may untwist at first, and it is suggested that each length is passed over a beeswax block before winding the bobbin. Use lengths of about 1 m on each bobbin.

1 · AUSTRALIAN BUTTERFLY
Duchesse lace

USE: a brooch

THREAD: Egyptian Cotton No. 60

146 The Australian Duchesse lace butterfly

TECHNIQUES
Cl st, h st, setting up a pointed edge, decorative filling, straight edge (four-about-the-pin edge) braid, dividing the sections, tally, picot, Bruges rib.

ORDER OF WORK
1 At (a) set up the body following Fig. 148, noting that continuous pairs are used, including the contour pairs. Work a four-about-the-pin edge braid and the centre filling as marked on Fig. 147. Gradually hang in more pairs symmetrically, until there are 16 pairs on the pillow. Stop working the veins 2 rows from the junction. Note the directional lines.
2 The body and thorax are divided by working the contour pairs, in cl st, to the opposite edges. Support the contour pair with a pin as close to the edge as you can. Do not put any strain on the contour pair. Twist each passive pair twice, and return the contour pair to its original position.
3 Work two rows of the thorax before starting to work the centre filling again.

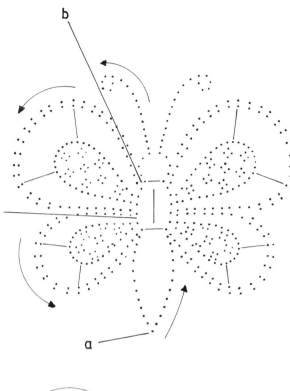

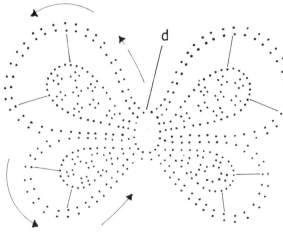

147 A three-dimensional Australian butterfly worked in Duchesse lace

4 The centre filling is worked to within two rows of the head junction. Divide the two sections as before, and work the head in cl st, throwing out four pairs.

5 Divide the remaining pairs into two equal groups. Each group, of six pairs, will be used to work a Bruges rib for the antennae. Sew out the pairs into the rib. Tie and cut off.

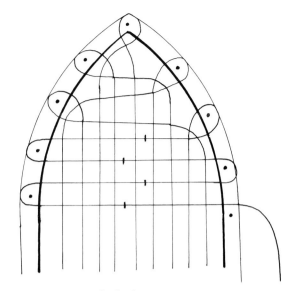

148 Setting up the body

The large wing

1 At (b) sew in five pairs, and hang in the contour pair, suspended from a pin at the rear of the work.

2 Work the cl st braid, with a Duchesse picot edge (Fig. 6), hanging in more pairs until there are 14 pairs on the pillow.

3 A thick line on the pricking shows where the sections are divided as described in Fig. 182. The middle section is worked in h st.

4 Work the last section as the first, throwing out pairs in the same order as they were added, until five pairs remain. Sew out, tie and cut off.

The small wing

1 At (c), immediately below the large wing, sew in five pairs and hang in the contour pair.

2 Work the small wing in a similar manner to the large wing, increasing to ten pairs only and working the sections alternately in cl st and h st as before.

3 Work the other pair of wings.

4 Work the tally filling (Fig. 84) in all the wings.

The under wings

1 At (d) put up a pin and hang on six pairs to work a Bruges rib around the inner curve of the thorax. Prior to the last three pins being worked, lay one pair to the back of the work. When all the pins are worked and the threads sewn in, knot each pair then place the remaining pairs to the back between these two threads. Using these two threads, tie them down to the lace firmly and cut off the threads.

2 Work the four wings as worked for the main section.

3 Place the top wings on top of the under wings of the butterfly and stab stitch the two together as close to the rib as possible. Open the wings, for flight, and spray with an unperfumed hair spray.

4 Allow the butterfly to dry. Attach a small gold safety pin to the body.

2 · AUSTRALIAN BUTTERFLY
Brussels tape lace

USE: decoration for a wine bottle apron with six coasters

THREADS AND MATERIALS: DMC Special Dentelles, 4 m narrow Brussels tape, iron-on Vilene, 25 cm brightly coloured plain fabric

149 The wine bottle apron, decorated in Brussels tape lace

TECHNIQUES
Twisted Russian, interwoven Russian, cluster insertion, bars.

PREPARATION
Prepare the design, etc. as described for the Brussels tape lace dragonfly (p. 21). Press the plain fabric and iron on the Vilene.

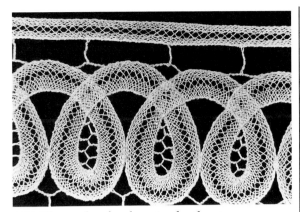

150 The pocket for the wine bottle apron

ORDER OF WORK
The apron
1 Study the patterns and suggested stitches carefully. The stitches are marked numerically:

(1) twisted Russian (Fig. 40);
(2) interwoven Russian (Fig. 143);
(3) cluster insertion (Fig. 144);
(4) bars (Fig. 152).

2 Work the bib of the apron, remembering to leave plenty of tape for the armholes, neck and tying. Note the small bars joining the edge to the looped section.

3 Work the pocket. Carefully mitre the corners symmetrically as the braid is tacked into position. Note the small bars.

4 Cut out the apron from the brightly coloured plain fabric. Tack on the tape down the LH edge, the lower edge and then the RH edge along the fitting line (Fig. 153).

5 Place the completed bib and pocket in position and tack in place.

6 Stab stitch through all thicknesses along each edge.

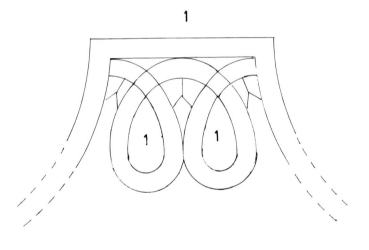

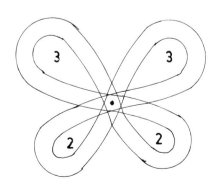

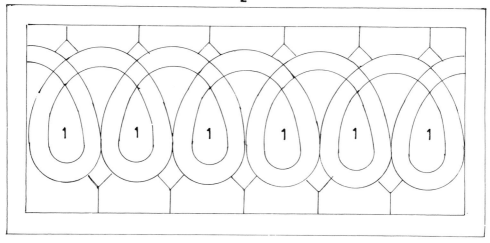

pocket

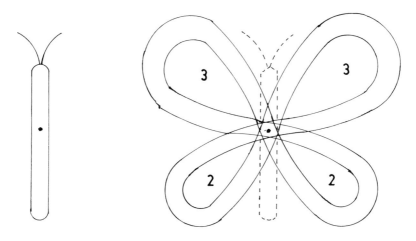

151 *A simple Brussels tape lace butterfly, which could be used to decorate a wine bottle apron holding coasters: bib and pocket design*

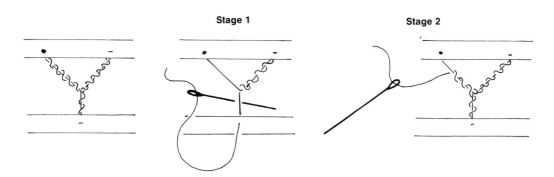

152 *Stages for working the whipped Y-bars*

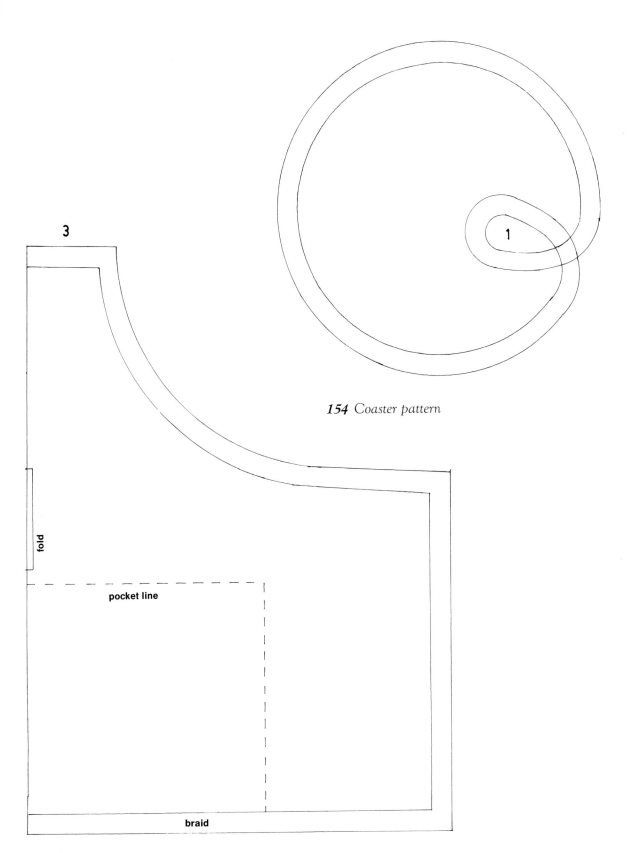

3

fold

pocket line

braid

154 Coaster pattern

1

153 Apron pattern

7 Cut away the plain fabric close to the edges of the braid. The Vilene will help to prevent fraying.
8 Work the six circular motifs for the coasters (Fig. 154). Tack each one on to the brightly coloured fabric. Finish each one as previously described.

The butterfly

Prepare the design, etc. as described for the Brussels tape lace dragonfly (p. 21).
1 Work the small three-dimensional butterfly. The fillings are marked numerically for identification and are the same as those used for the main apron.

155 The Australian Brussels tape lace butterfly

2 The antennae are worked with buttonhole stitches over two laid threads.
3 Stitch the small section over the larger section, and then both to the body.
4 The butterfly may be attached to the bib or to the pocket of the apron.

3 · AUSTRALIAN BUTTERFLY
Irish lace

USE: a placemat

THREADS AND MATERIALS: DMC Retors d'Alsace/Broder Machine Nos 30 and 50, DMC Coton Perlé No. 12, organdie, coarse tulle, architect's paper, cover cloth, ballpoint needles

156 An Irish lace placemat, worked with the Australian butterfly motif

TECHNIQUES
Couching, seeds/pops, twirling.

PREPARATION
Prepare the organdie and tulle as described for the Irish lace bee (p. 12).

ORDER OF WORK
1 Couch along the design lines of the pattern the outer and inner circles, the body and wings of the butterfly.
2 Carefully take out the tacking threads and cut away the unwanted organdie only.
3 Re-tack around the antennae, and couch over the remaining design lines.
4 Note the position of the seeds/pops and work them (Fig. 44).
5 Work the twirling (Fig. 46) around the outer edge, keeping each 'twirl' the same size.

6 Cut away the unwanted organdie and tulle under the twirling.

7 Remove the tacking threads. Press the lace on the WS, protecting it with a damp linen cloth. Finish off any remaining threads on reverse of work.

157 The Australian butterfly worked in Irish lace

4 · AUSTRALIAN BUTTERFLY
needle lace

USE: a brooch

THREADS: DMC Special Dentelles No. 80, horsehair for the cordonnette, wire for the cordonnette of the top wing

---

TECHNIQUES

Main butterfly: single corded Brussels with vein eye, single corded Brussels with two four-pin buds and three veins to point, Point de Venise, spaced single Brussels, four rows oval space filling with herringbone to fill the space, single Brussels, eight-legged spider, five Alençon bars on one row single Brussels.
Top wings: Point de Venise, eight-legged spider, six Alençon bars on one row single Brussels, single Brussels, wheel insertion.

PREPARATION
Prepare the design, etc. as described for the needle lace bee (p. 15).

ORDER OF WORK
The fillings are marked numerically for identification.

Main butterfly
(1) single corded Brussels with vein eye (Fig. 161); and grid (Fig. 167);
(2) single corded Brussels (Fig. 27) with two four-pin buds and three veins to point (grid for bud and vein, Fig. 167;)
(3) Point de Venise (Fig. 162);
(4) spaced single Brussels (Fig. 163);
(5) four rows of oval space filling with herringbone to fill the space (Fig. 164);
(6) single Brussels (Fig. 25);
(7) eight-legged spider (Fig. 165);
(8) five Alençon bars on one row single Brussels (Fig. 166).

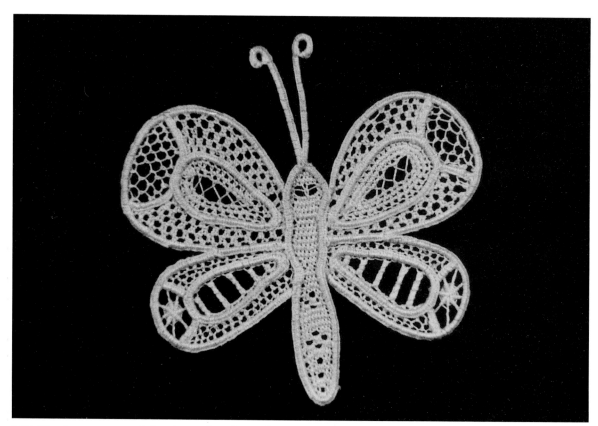

158 The lower wings of the Australian butterfly

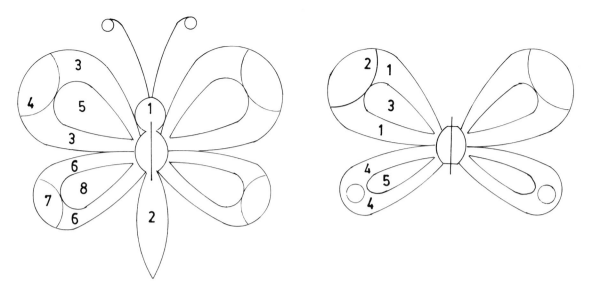

159 & 160 *The Australian butterfly worked in three-dimensional needle lace*

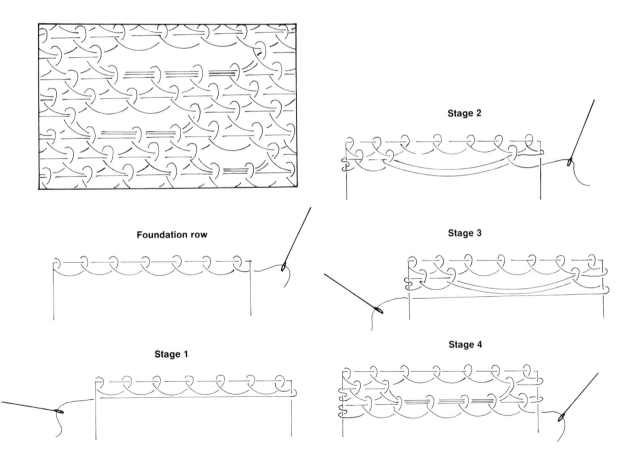

Stage 2

Stage 3

Stage 4

Foundation row

Stage 1

161 *Stages for working single corded Brussels with vein eye*

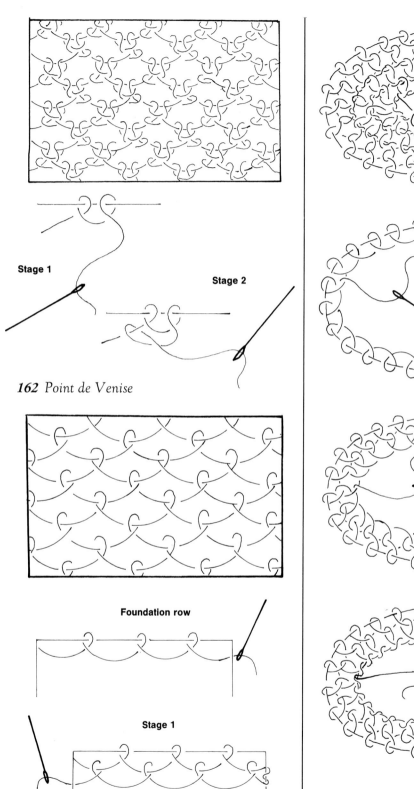

Stage 1

Stage 2

162 Point de Venise

Foundation row

Stage 1

163 Spaced single Brussels filling

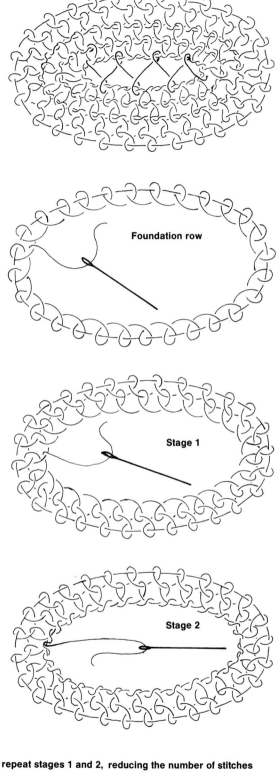

Foundation row

Stage 1

Stage 2

repeat stages 1 and 2, reducing the number of stitches
to accommodate the curve

164 Four-row oval filled with herringbone

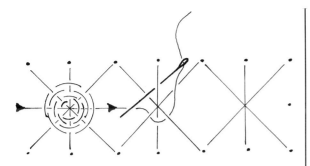

165 *Eight-legged spider insertions, untwisted legs*

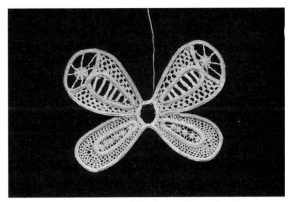

167 *The top wings of the brooch ready for mounting*

Top wings

(1) Point de Venise (Fig. 162);
(2) eight-legged untwisted spider insertion (Fig. 165);
(3) six Alençon bars on one row single Brussels (Fig. 166);
(4) single Brussels (Fig. 25);
(5) eight-legged twisted spider insertion (Fig. 55).

COMPLETION

Antennae are made by close buttonhole stitches over four threads anchoring the first stitch to prevent sliding off the cordonet (Fig. 169). Work as instructed for the needle lace bee (p. 19). To assemble as brooch, follow instructions as for Duchesse lace butterfly brooch.

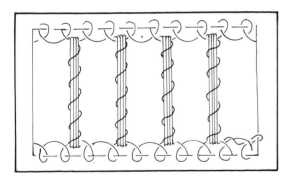

Foundation rows

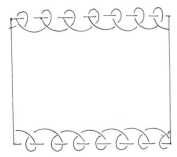

166 *Twisted bars*

Stage 1

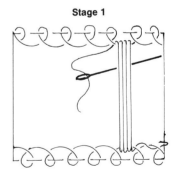

Stage 2

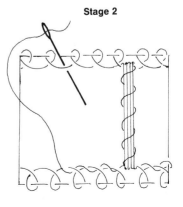

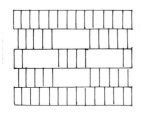

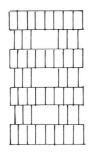

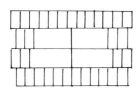

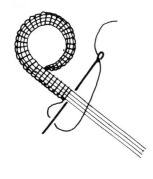

168 Grid for working spaces and eyes

169 Antennae workings

5 · AUSTRALIAN BUTTERFLY
tatted lace

USE: a mobile

THREAD AND TOOLS: DMC Special Dentelles No. 80, No. 60 crochet hook, tatting shuttle

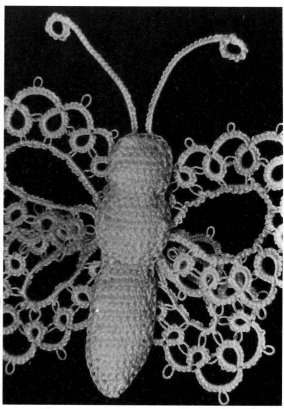

170 The crocheted body and single wings of the tatted Australian butterfly

TECHNIQUES
Picot (p), double stitch (d), close ring (cl r), reverse work (RW); double crochet (d c), ring (r), chain (ch).

ORDER OF WORK
The large wing
1 R of 3 d, 3 p, separated by 3 d, 3 d, cl r.
2 RW. Ch, 4 d, 1 p, 4 d.
3 RW. 3 d, join to last p of last r, 3 d, 1 p, 3 d, 1 p, 3 d, cl r.

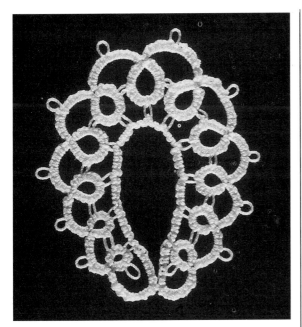

171 The large tatted wing

4 RW. Ch. 4 d, 1 p, 4 d.
5 RW. R, 4 d, join to last p of last r, 4 d,
1 p, 4 d, 1 p, 4 d, cl r.
6 RW. Ch, 5 d, 1 p, 5 d.
7 RW. R, 5 d, join to last p of the last r, 5 d,
1 p, 5 d, 1 p, 5 d, cl r.
8 RW. Ch, 6 d, 1 p, 6 d. RW. R. 5 d, join to
last p of last r, 5 d, 1 p, 5 d, 1 p, 5 d, cl r.
9 RW. Ch, 6 d, 1 p, 6 d. RW. R. 6 d, join to
last p of the last r, 6 d, 1 p, 6 d, 1 p, 6 d, cl r.
10 RW. Ch, 6 d, 1 p, 6 d.
11 RW. R, 5 d, join to last p of last r, 5 d,
1 p, 5 d, 1 p, 5 d, cl r.
12 RW. Ch, 6 d, 1 p, 6 d. RW. R. 5 d, join
to last p of last r, 5 d, 1 p, 5 d, 1 p, 5 d, cl r.
13 RW. Ch, 5 d, 1 p, 5 d. RW. R. 4 d, join
to last p of last r, 4 d, 1 p, 4 d, 1 p, 4 d, cl r.
14 RW. Ch, 4 d, 1 p, 4 d. RW. 3 d, join to
last p of last r, 3 d, 1p, 3 d, 1 p, 3 d, cl r.
15 RW. 4 d, 1 p, 4 d. RW, R, 3 d, join to
last p of last r, 3 d, 1 p, 3 d, 1 p, 3 d, cl r.
16 RW. Ch, 14 d, join to second p of the
last r, *4 d, join to second p of next r*.
17 Repeat from * to * twice. 3 d, join to
second p of the next r. **2 d, join to second
p of the next r**. Repeat from ** to ** once. 3
d, join to second p of next r. ***4 d, join to
second p of next r***.

18 Repeat from *** to *** twice. 14 d. Cut
the threads, leaving enough to sew shuttle
thread into the base of first r. Tie and sew
the shuttle thread neatly back over 8 of 14 d.
19 Join to the first 14 d, at 8th d, and leave
ready to sew into the body of the butterfly.
20 Finish the ball thread off by sewing neatly
into first r. Repeat three times more to make
the four wings.

The small wing
1 R of 3 d, 3 p, separated by 3 d, 3 d, cl r.
2 RW. Ch, *4 d, 1 p, 4 d.
3 RW. R, 3 d, join to last p of last r, 3 d,
1 p, 3 d, 1 p, 3 d, cl r*.
4 Repeat from * to * twice.
5 RW. Ch, 7 d, 1 p, 7 d. RW. R, 6 d, join to
last p of last r, 3 d, 1 p, 3 d, 1 p, 6 d, cl r.
6 RW. Ch, 7 d, 1 p, 7 d. **RW. R. 3 d, join
to last p of last r, 3 d, 1 p, 3 d, 1 p, 3 d, cl r.
RW. Ch, 4 d, 1 p, 4 d**.
7 Repeat from ** to ** twice.
8 RW. R, 3 d, join to last p of last r, 3 d, 1
p, 3 d, 1 p, 3 d, cl r.
9 RW. Ch, 14 d, join to 2nd p of the last r,
(4 d, join to second p of the next r) twice. (2
d, join to second p of the next r) twice. (4 d,
join to 2nd p of the next r) three times.
10 14 d, cut and sew the threads into the
base of the first r. Work back to the eighth
d, by sewing in one thread, and join to the
eighth d of the first 14 d.
11 Leave a length of thread to join to the
butterfly body. Work three more wings in a
similar manner.

The body
1 Follow Fig. 172, using d c for each square.
2 Work two bodies, join together with a row
of d c, and pad evenly with cotton wool.
3 The antennae are worked by working 40 d,
curved round and sewn into the antennae to
form a ring.

MOUNTING
1 Sew the four large and four small wings
together in pairs. Place the body over the top
of them and stab stitch them together. The
wings may be stiffened with boiled sugar (two
tablespoons) and water (one or two

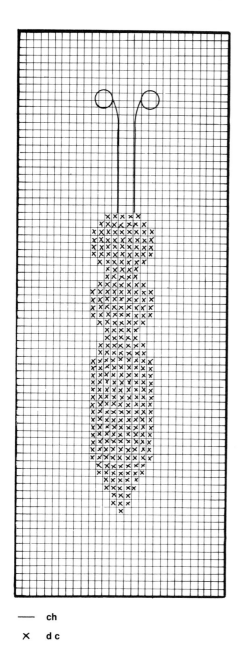

— ch
× d c

172 The tatted butterfly, the body crocheted and then padded

tablespoons). The solution is painted on the lace and allowed to dry thoroughly before assembly. Single wings may be used.
2 Thread two beads on to a needle and thread. Pass needle and thread through the body so that the butterfly will hang as though in flight.

6 · HONG KONG BUTTERFLY
Bruges flower lace

USE: hairbrush and mirror

THREADS: DMC Retors d'Alsace/Broder Machine No. 50, shade Nos 350 (red), 310 (black), white, sand, 944 grey

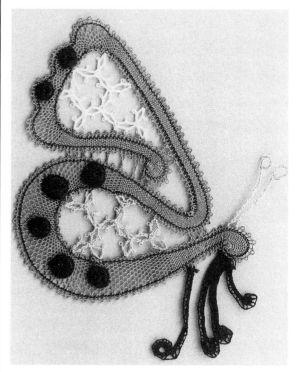

173 The Hong Kong butterfly worked in Bruges flower lace

TECHNIQUES
Cl st, b st, h st, Bruges rib, d st edge, starting and finishing a scroll, hanging in a pair, sewings, plait-with-picot filling, couronne or sequin.

ORDER OF WORK
1 At (a) (Fig. 174), using shade 350, set up the scroll (Fig. 175). Include a pair of black threads (as contour threads) at each side of the work (Fig. 176).

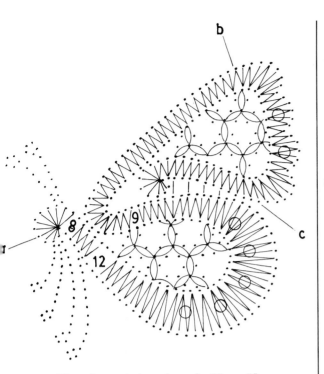

174 *This design is based on the Hong Kong stamp, worked in Bruges flower lace*

176 *Detail of the Hong Kong Bruges flower lace butterfly*

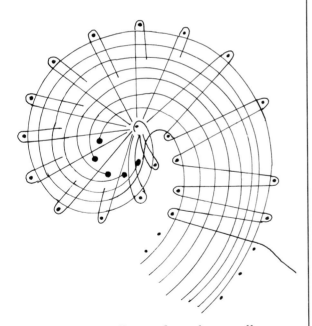

175 *Setting up a Bruges flower lace scroll*

2 Increase to eight pairs as the scroll is worked. It will be necessary to increase to 12 pairs before the plait-with-picot pinmark is worked. Change to h st and note the b st worked around the curve.

3 Observe Fig. 173 to see where the stitch changes back to cl st. Gradually reduce the pairs to nine. Several b sts should be worked around the curve.
4 At pin (b), change to h st, to work the shaped edge. Each section is separated with a row of d st, worked from the outer to the inner edge.
5 At pin (c) change to cl st. Note the false plaits (Fig. 67) and sewings.
6 The motif is completed by working a scroll (Fig. 127).
7 Using white thread for the upper wing and sand-coloured thread for the lower wing, work the plait-with-picot filling (Fig. 69).
8 The legs are worked in Bruges rib (Fig. 5), using shade 310 (start at the feet), and the antennae are worked in plaits, using shade 944 (grey).
9 Needle lace couronnes or sequins can be stitched on to wing to finish.

7 · HONG KONG BUTTERFLY
Duchesse lace

USE: a mobile

THREADS AND MATERIALS: Egyptian Cotton No. 60, DMC Coton Perlé No. 12 (white), 25 cm oval frame

177 The Hong Kong Duchesse lace butterfly

TECHNIQUES
Cl st, h st, b st, straight edge (four-about-the-pin edge) braid, hanging in/throwing out pairs, setting up and finishing a scroll, Bruges rib, dividing the petals, picot, plait-with-picot, raised edge.

ORDER OF WORK
The body
1 At (a) (Fig. 178) put up a pin. Hang on nine pairs, a double contour pair and a double edge pair (Fig. 134). One contour pair and one edge pair are left to work the other edge

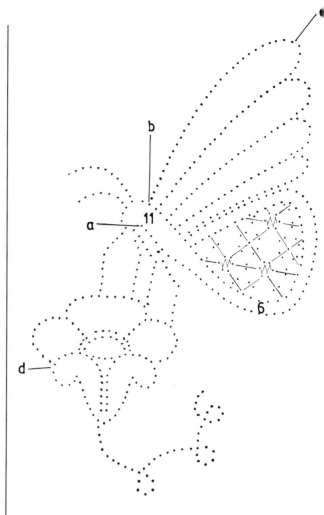

178 Duchesse lace has been selected to work the Hong Kong butterfly

of the braid when the scroll is finished. Very small holes will appear as the scroll is worked (Fig. 134).
2 Work this braid in cl st, using a four-about-the-pin edge.
3 As the cl st braid narrows, gradually throw out five pairs. Complete the cl st braid with the six pairs. B st must be worked to accommodate the curves.
4 Sew out into the edge of the braid, tie and cut off the threads.

The top wings
1 Each section is raised. Figs 178 and 179 should be constantly observed.
2 At (b) sew in five pairs. From a pin at the rear of the work hang on a contour pair.

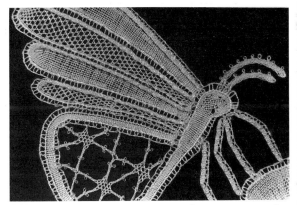

179 Raised work, the filling and antennae used to work the Hong Kong Duchesse lace butterfly

3 Following Fig. 178, work the Bruges rib until (c) and turn the curve (Figs 180a & b). Use whichever pinholes are necessary for this wing. The number of pinholes required will be defined by the size of the wing. One more pair may be added if required.
4 Work the wing in cl st, sewing into the bottom bar of each pinloop, and over the rib (11 pairs).
5 Complete the wing, gradually throwing out five pairs as the wing narrows. Sew out six pairs into the body. Complete the wings as described for working the Duchesse lace cockerel (p. 72). The wings may be worked alternately in cl st and h st.
6 Finally, when working the last wing, sewings are made into the braid below this wing. Sew out into the body.

The scrolls and flower
1 Work the RH scroll first (Fig. 134), using nine pairs and a double contour pair and edge pair. Throw out three pairs as the braid narrows.
2 Turn the base using b st (pivoting on a pin). Work the short length of braid, hanging in three pairs. Sewings are made to hold the two braids together in the centre.
3 Finish the scroll following Fig. 134.
4 At (d), sew in 12 pairs. Use the pinloops and the bar between the loops to make the sewings.
5 Follow Fig. 181. Note the direction of the worker line, and how the pairs are

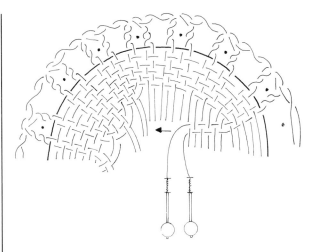

180a Working a curved raised cl st edge

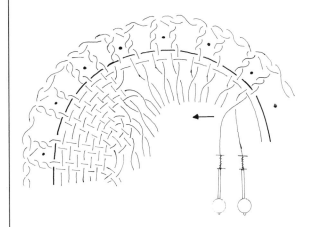

180b Working a curved raised h st edge

introduced into the lace. Also note the extra pinholes needed to work the petals.
6 Each petal is divided as shown in Fig. 182.
7 Sew out the threads in the same order as they were hung in. Tie and cut off.

The legs
1 Using six pairs, work each leg in Bruges rib (Fig. 5). Set up by sewing into the braid edge of the flower and sew out into the body. The pin edge faces the front.

The antennae
1 Work the antennae in Bruges rib and picot (Figs 5 and 6).

The filling
1 Following Fig. 136, work the filling using a

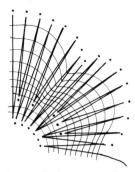

181 Extra pinholes needed to work the petals

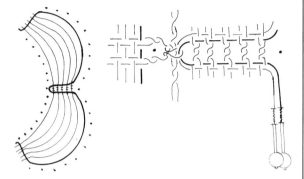

182 Dividing the petals

plait-with-picot and a h st bud. Count the number of h st worked in each half of the plait. Sew out the plaits only. When all the plaits are sewn out, firm them all, tie and cut off all the threads.

The tendril

1 Using six pairs, work the Bruges rib, keeping the pins to the left. Picots at intervals may be used to decorate the tendril.

COMPLETION
Mount for a mobile if desired.

8 · HONG KONG BUTTERFLY
Irish lace

USE: a placemat

THREADS AND MATERIALS: DMC Retors d'Alsace/Broder Machine Nos 30 and 50, DMC Coton Perlé No. 12, organdie, coarse tulle, cover cloth, architect's paper, ballpoint needles

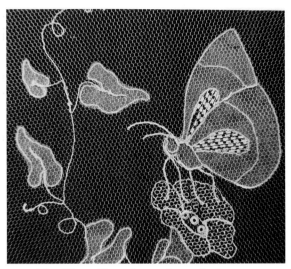

183 The Hong Kong butterfly worked in Irish lace, showing details of the wrong side securing of threads

TECHNIQUES
Couching, twirling, seed/pops, Irish lace filling No. 1 (variation) and 3.

PREPARATION
Prepare the organdie and tulle as described for the Irish lace bee (p. 12).

ORDER OF WORK
1 Couch the design lines around the two outer circles, the whole of the butterfly (not the legs or the antennae), the leaves and the calyx. Remove the tacking threads around the design lines.
2 Cut away only the unwanted organdie, so that the flower, stems, legs and antennae may be worked. Tack close to the remaining

184 A placemat, worked in Irish lace, the design
based upon the Hong Kong stamp

design lines. Do not cut away the fabric around the outer edge.

3 Seeds/pops (Fig. 44) are worked in the centre of the flower, Irish lace filling No. 3 (Fig. 43) in the flower and Irish lace filling No. 6 (variation) (Fig. 185) in the wings. Work the antennae and the legs over the petals, couching over a double thickness of Coton Perlé.

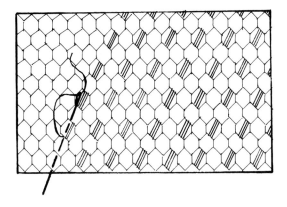

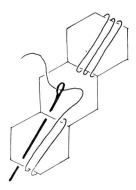

185 Irish lace filling No. 6

4 Work the twirling (Fig. 46) around the outer edge, keeping each 'twirl' the same size. Cut away the fabrics under the twirling.
5 Remove all the tacking threads and press the lace on the WS, using a slightly damp linen cloth to protect the lace.

9 · HUNGARIAN BUTTERFLY
Russian tape lace

USE: a cushion cover

THREADS: DMC Retors d'Alsace/Broder Machine No. 30, shade Nos 310 (black), 744 (yellow) and pale blue, Gütermann black/silver gimp thread

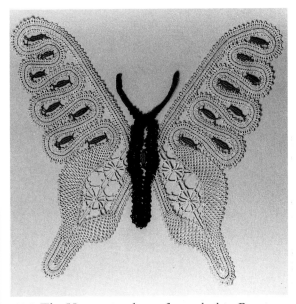

186 The Hungarian butterfly worked in Russian tape lace

TECHNIQUES
Cl st, d st, d st edge, simple edge braid, sewings, hanging in/throwing out a pair, leaf plait, pivoting on a pin (b st), Bruges rib.

ORDER OF WORK
The body
1 At (a) (Fig. 187) put up a pin. Hang on five pairs, wound in black thread.
2 Working in the Bruges rib technique (Fig. 5), work down towards the head. Place the pin to the LH edge.
3 At (b) change to a d st edge braid on the outer edge and a simple edge braid on the inner edge. Hang in two more pairs as the braid widens.

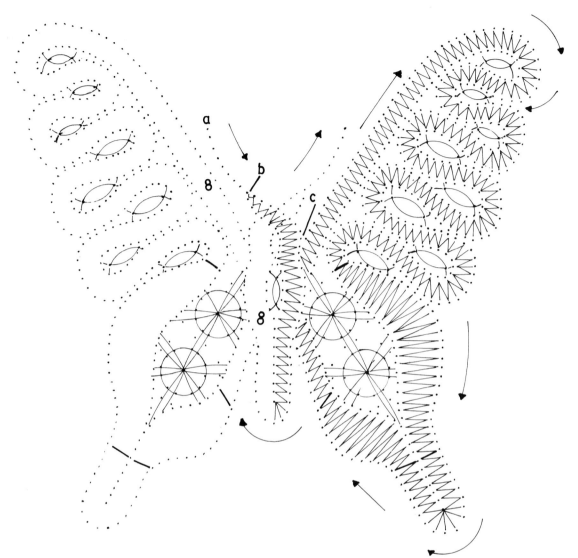

187 Russian tape lace provides an ideal braid and filling to work this butterfly

4 Hang in the Gütermann gimp thread, working the Russian tape lace braid (Fig. 73). Work the braid and sewings in the tail section and one sewing at the junction of the head and thorax.

5 Cross the braid, working the sewings into the appropriate pinloops. Throw out two pairs as the braid narrows (five pairs on the pillow). Note the directional lines.

6 Work the antennae in Bruges rib. When the second to last pin has been worked lay one of the centre pairs to the back of the work. Finish working the rib, firm all the pairs, and open out the pair laid to the back.

7 Place the four pairs to the back of the work between the two threads. Tie them three times and cut off the threads.

8 Work the leaf plait within the body, using the red DMC Retors d'Alsace thread.

The RH wing

1 At (c) set up the wings. Note the worker lines and gradually, as the rows are worked, hang in seven yellow pairs and one pair of Gütermann gimp threads in the centre.

2 Take care when working the curved areas to work the b st, and the sewings.

3 You will notice the thick line marked across the braid and the directional arrows. Here the Gütermann gimp is laid aside in order to work the next section in h st. This gimp is introduced again to work the short length of braid at the tip of the lower wing, laid aside again to work the braid in h st, and finally introduced to work the last section of the braid.

4 The threads are gradually sewn out into the body of the butterfly.

5 Using a red DMC Retors d'Alsace/Broder Machine thread, work the leaf plaits inside the curves of the wing.

The LH wing

1 Using the same threads and techniques, work the other wing. The order of work will be reversed from that of the RH wing.

The wing filling

1 Observe the filling which has been selected for use (Fig. 77). Work it in each section of the wing, using a pale blue Gütermann thread.

10 · HUNGARIAN BUTTERFLY
Irish lace

USE: a placemat

THREADS AND MATERIALS: DMC Retors d'Alsace/Broder Machine Nos 30 and 50, Coton Perlé No. 12, organdie, coarse tulle, architect's paper, cover cloth, ballpoint needle

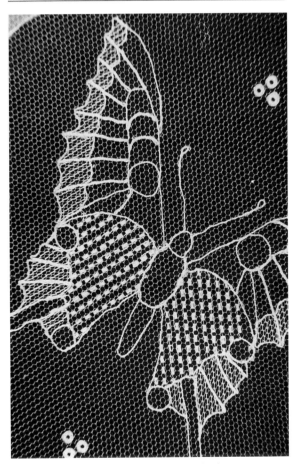

188 *The Hungarian butterfly worked in Irish lace*

TECHNIQUES

Couching, seeds/pops, twirling, Irish lace filling Nos 1 and 6.

PREPARATION

Prepare the organdie and tulle as described for the Irish lace bee (p. 12).

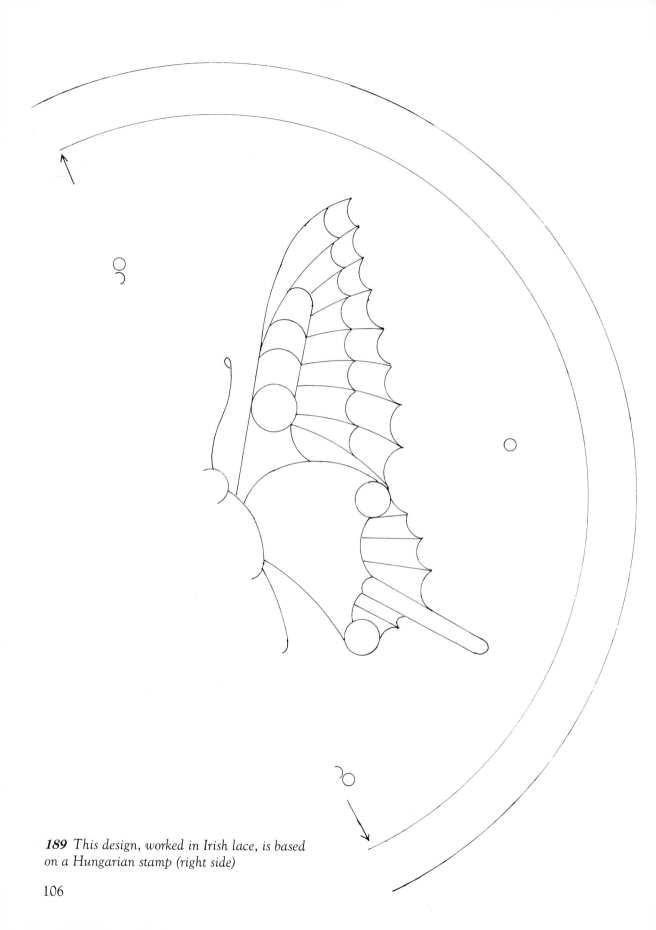

189 This design, worked in Irish lace, is based on a Hungarian stamp (right side)

ORDER OF WORK

1 Tack the two layers of fabric on to the cover cloth close to the two outer circles. Using the finer thread in a ballpoint needle, couch the Coton Perlé thread around the two outer circles and around edges of wings.

2 Remove the tacking threads and cut away the organdie from the inner circle edge only.

3 Tack close to the design lines of the butterfly.

4 Observe the design (Fig. 189) and plan well in advance the route you will follow in couching the design. The top LH and RH wings are easier to work if the lines are worked with one continuous thread. This will give a double line of couching in some places, and will cut down the number of threads requiring finishing off when the lace is completed.

5 The large space in the lower wings is worked in Irish lace filling No. 6 (Fig. 185) and the small areas at the edges of the wings may be worked in Irish lace filling No. 1 (Fig. 18), using the coarser Broder Machine thread. Work the seed/pops (Fig. 44) where marked on the pattern.

6 Work the twirling (Fig. 46) around the outer circle edge, keeping the twirls all the same size.

7 Carefully cut away the two layers of fabric from under the twirling.

COMPLETION

Finish off the work as described for the Irish lace bee (p. 14).

11 · HUNGARIAN MOTH
torchon lace

USE: a mobile

THREADS AND MATERIALS: Bouc linen 100/2 white, 48 pairs; DMC Coton Perlé No. 8 (black) for the gimp, two pairs; metal mobile frame 30 × 11 cm

TECHNIQUES

Torchon ground, spiders, roseground, passing a gimp thread, footing.

ORDER OF WORK

1 Set up in a similar manner as for the torchon guest towels (p. 45). The same two pairs of passive threads will run along all four of the edges.

2 Start to work the torchon ground at the top LH corner. Introduce one pair of threads, from the two pairs previously hung, into each diagonal row.

3 At (a) (Fig. 192) the first gimp is hung in to work the roseground rings and the second one is hung in at (b). The two gimps remain

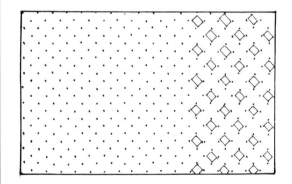

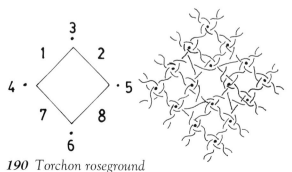

190 Torchon roseground

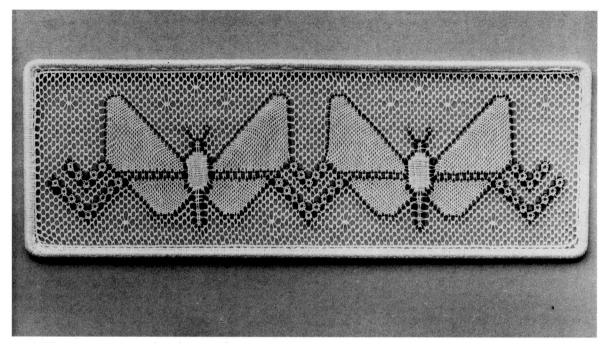

191 *The Hungarian torchon lace moth*

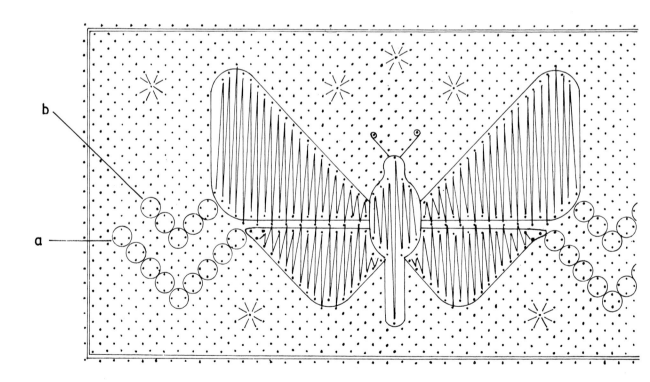

192 *The moth, worked in torchon lace, mounted as a mobile*

continuous, working around the body, the antennae, the wings and straight through to the far end of the design. Consult the notes for passing the gimps (p. 30).

4 Finish the gimps off by passing them between the threads of the circles.

5 The last row of the design is completed in the same way as for the torchon guest towels (p. 46).

MOUNTING

1 Cover the metal frame by blanket stitching firmly and closely over the metal edges of the frame.

2 Oversew the edge of the blanket-stitched frame to the footing edges of the lace. The lace must be stretched on to the frame for a good result.

3 Stitch the hanging cord in place.

12 · HUNGARIAN MOTH
Irish lace

USE: a placemat

THREADS AND MATERIALS: DMC Retors d'Alsace/Broder Machine Nos 30 and 50, Coton Perlé No. 12, organdie, coarse tulle, cover cloth, architect's paper, ballpoint needles

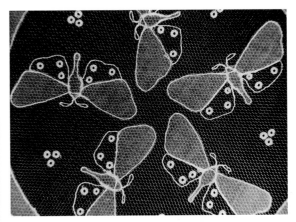

193 The Hungarian moth worked in Irish lace

TECHNIQUES
Couching, seeds/pops, twirling.

PREPARATION
Prepare the organdie and tulle as described for the Irish lace bee (p. 12).

ORDER OF WORK

1 Look at the finished placemat (Fig. 193) and note where the organdie and stitches are used. Couch around the two outer circles, the upper wings, and the body of the moth. Remove the tacking threads.

2 Cut away the organdie from the inner edge of the circle, the lower wings and the body. Tack around the edges of the moth again, and couch the edges of the lower wings and the antennae.

3 Work all the seeds/pops (Fig. 44) in the lower wings of the moth and the groups of three seeds/pops.

194a *A simple design, based on the Hungarian stamp, used on a placemat (left side)*

4 Work the twirling (Fig. 46) around the outer edge of the circle. Keep the twirls the same size. Cut away the organdie and tulle from underneath the twirling.

COMPLETION
Finish off the work as described for the Irish lace bee (p. 14).

13 · ANTIGUAN BUTTERFLY
Duchesse lace

USE: decoration for a workbag

THREADS: Madeira Embroidery Thread, shade Nos 550, 552, 553, 554, black (one single thread used with one single thread of another shade)

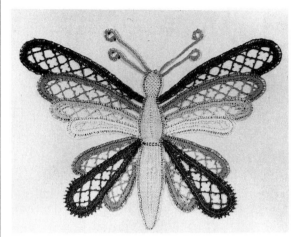

195 *The Antiguan butterfly worked in Duchesse lace*

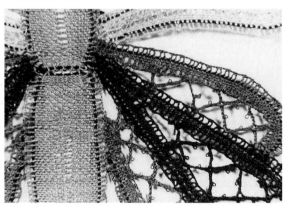

196 *The rear wings and the body of the Antiguan Duchesse lace butterfly*

TECHNIQUES
Cl st, h st, plait-with-picot, Bruges rib, crossing of contour threads, setting up a curved edge, sewings, tying off several threads, a ladder, straight-edge (four-about-the-pin edge) braid, hanging in and throwing out a pair, Duchesse picot.

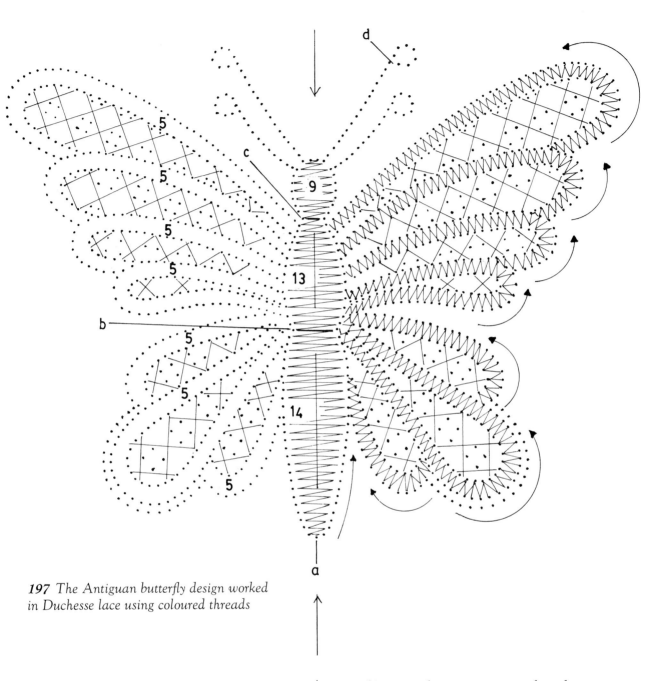

*197 The Antiguan butterfly design worked
in Duchesse lace using coloured threads*

ORDER OF WORK

1 At (a) (Fig. 197) and using shade 553, set
up the curved edge (Fig. 33). One black and
one 553 thread are used as contour pairs. A
ladder, formed by twisting the worker pair
twice, decorates the centre of the body and
thorax.

2 Gradually hang in more pairs until there
are 14 pairs on the pillow.

3 At (b), cross the contour pairs, by taking
them from one side to the other (p. 30) and
work the thorax, using 13 pairs for this
section.

4 As the thorax narrows throw out four
pairs and cross the contour pairs as before at
(c).

5 Work the head in h st, reducing to six
pairs, carefully keeping the contour line.

6 Fasten off the threads by working a cl st with the contour threads and the edge pairs. Tie each pair. Open out a pair which has been thrown out, and lay all the pairs between these threads. Tie this pair into a reef knot. Cut off the threads.

7 Starting at (d) each time, work the antennae in Bruges rib, sewing out into the head.

The upper wings

1 The small, lower section, using shade 554, is worked first in a four-about-the-pin edge braid. A black contour pair is used (five pairs altogether). Sewings are made at the centre of the wing. Note the directional arrows.

2 Work the other three sections using shades 553, 552 and 550. Set up the sections by sewing into the previously worked braid and sewing out into the edge of the body braid.

3 Work the plait-with-picot filling (Fig. 74) in the wings.

The lower wings

1 Work the centre section first, using shade 550, four pairs and one contour pair and the same braid as before. Note the directional arrows and picot edge.

2 Work the LH and RH sections, using shade 552, setting up by making the sewings into the centre wing each time.

3 Work the plait-with-picot filling in the wings.

14 · ANTIGUAN BUTTERFLY
Brussels tape lace

USE: skirt pocket decoration

THREADS AND TAPE: DMC Special Dentelles, 3 m narrow Brussels tape

198 *The Antiguan butterfly worked in Brussels tape lace*

TECHNIQUES

Spider, single and double Brussels, Brussels Russian, four laid threads buttonholed.

PREPARATION

Prepare the design, etc. as described for the Brussels tape lace dragonfly (p. 21).

ORDER OF WORK

1 Study the design and suggested stitches carefully (Fig. 201). The stitches are marked numerically:
(1) Brussels six-legged spider (Fig. 201);
(2) single Brussels (Fig. 25);
(3) double Brussels (Fig. 120);
(4) Russian (Fig. 142);
(5) four laid threads, buttonholed (Fig. 169).

2 Finish the work as described for the Brussels tape lace dragonfly (p. 23). Press the lace under a damp linen cloth.

3 Hem the lace to the pocket around the outer edges.

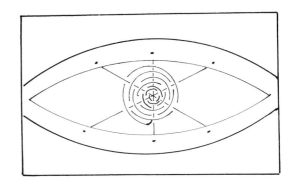

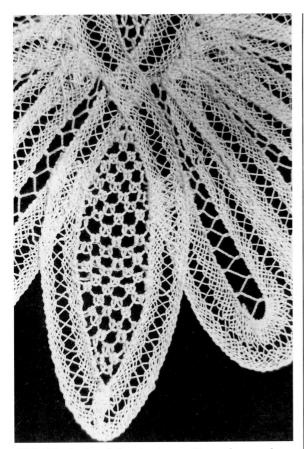

199 The body of the Antiguan Brussels tape lace
butterfly (detail)

200 The wings of the Antiguan Brussels tape
lace butterfly (detail)

Foundation threads

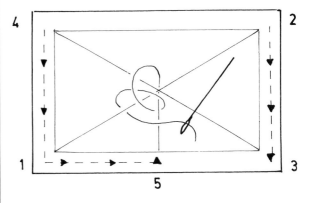

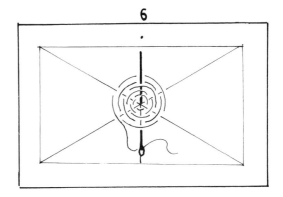

201 Brussels six-legged sider

115

202 *The Antiguan Brussels tape lace butterfly*

15 · ANTIGUAN BUTTERFLY
Irish lace

USE: a placemat

THREADS AND MATERIALS: DMC
Retors d'Alsace/Broder Machine Nos 30 and
50, DMC Coton Perlé No. 12, organdie,
coarse tulle, architect's paper, cover cloth,
ballpoint needles

203 *An Irish lace placemat using the Antiguan butterfly motif*

TECHNIQUES
Couching, twirling, seeds/pops, Irish lace
filling Nos 4 (variation), 6 and 7.

PREPARATION
Prepare the organdie and tulle as described
for the Irish lace bee (p. 12).

ORDER OF WORK
1 Using the finer thread in a needle, couch
(Fig. 17) the Coton Perlé over the two outer
circle design lines (Fig. 205).
2 Take out the tacking threads and cut away
the organdie from the centre of the placemat.
3 Tack close to the design lines of the
butterfly. Couch over the design lines of the
butterfly.
4 In the sections marked No. 1, work Irish
lace filling No. 6 (Fig. 185); in the section
marked No. 2, work Irish lace filling No. 7
(Fig. 204). The thorax is worked in Irish lace
filling No. 4 (variation) (Fig. 94).
5 Work the seeds/pops (Fig. 44) at the tips
of the wings and as marked on the tulle.
6 Work the twirling around the edge,
keeping the twirls all the same size. Cut away
the organdie and tulle under the twirling.

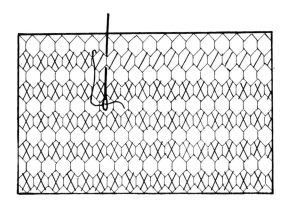

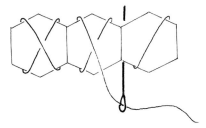

204 *Irish lace filling No. 7*

COMPLETION
Finish off the work as described for the Irish
lace bee (p. 14).

205 *A placemat using the Antiguan butterfly motif worked in Irish lace (right side)*

16 · ANTIGUAN BUTTERFLY
needle lace

USE: a brooch

THREADS AND MATERIALS: Egyptian Cotton No. 70, horsehair, florist's white wire

207 The upper wings of the Antiguan needle lace butterfly

ORDER OF WORK
1 Plan out the laying of the cordonnet well in advance (Fig. 208). Use two strands for the cordonnet and a finer thread in a needle to lay the cordonnet. Remember to keep the couching threads 2 mm apart, and it may be necessary to divide the two threads and retrace the line with the same thread to give a two-thread thickness again. The main butterfly and top wings are worked in the same manner.

2 The fillings are marked numerically for identification:
(1) corded single Brussels with two eyes (Fig. 27);
(2) corded single Brussels with veins (Fig. 27);
(3) pea stitch (Fig. 24);
(4) pea stitch variation (Fig. 28);
(5) whipped single Brussels (Fig. 209);
(6) double Brussels (Fig. 120);
(7) corded double Brussels (Fig. 210).

206 The lower wings of the Antiguan needle lace butterfly

TECHNIQUES
Laying the cordonnet, corded single Brussels, pea stitch, pea stitch variations, double Brussels, corded double Brussels, whipped single Brussels, cordonnette.

PREPARATION
Prepare the design, etc. as described for the needle lace bee (p. 15).

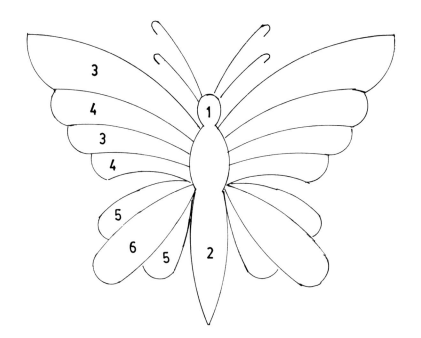

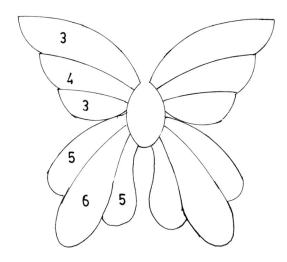

208 The Antiguan needle lace butterfly

3 Work the cordonnette (Fig. 30), using horsehair in the main butterfly. Use four strands of Egyptian Cotton, plus one wire to work the cordonnette around the top wings.

COMPLETION
Finish the work as described for the needle lace bee (p. 15). Stab stitch the upper wings to the body of the main butterfly. Sew a small safety pin to the underside of the body. Open the wings to give a three-dimensional effect.

Foundation row

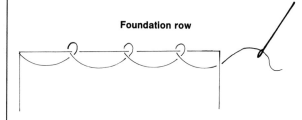

Stage 1

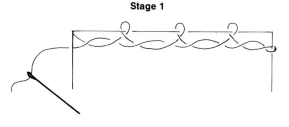

209 Whipped single Brussels filling

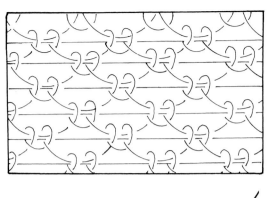

Foundation row

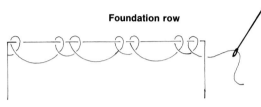

Stage 1

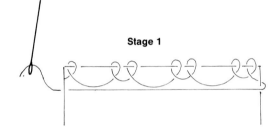

Stage 2

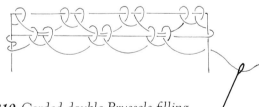

210 Corded double Brussels filling

SUPPLIERS AND SOURCES OF INFORMATION

GENERAL SUPPLIERS

UNITED KINGDOM

Alby Lace Museum
Cromer Road
Alby
Norwich
Norfolk NR11 7QE

Busy Bobbins
Unit 7
Scarrots Lane
Newport
Isle of Wight PO30 1JD

Chosen Crafts Centre
46 Winchcombe Street
Cheltenham
Gloucestershire GL52
 2ND

Jo Firth
Lace Marketing &
 Needlecraft Supplies
58 Kent Crescent
Lowtown
Pudsey
West Yorkshire LS28
 9EB

J. & J. Ford
October Hill
Upper Way
Upper Longdon
Rugeley
Staffordshire WS15 1QB

Framecraft
83 Hampstead Road
Handsworth Wood
Birmingham B2 1JA

R. Gravestock
Highwood
Crews Hill
Alfrick
Worcestershire WR6
 5HF

The Handicraft Shop
47 Northgate
Canterbury
Kent CT1 1BE

Frank Herring & Sons
26 High West Street
Dorchester
Dorset DT1 1UP

Honiton Lace Shop
44 High Street
Honiton
Devon

D. J. Hornsby
149 High Street
Burton Latimer
Kettering
Northamptonshire NN15
 5RL
 also at:
25 Manwood Avenue
Canterbury
Kent CT2 7AH

Frances Iles
73 High Street
Rochester
Kent ME1 1LX

Jane's Pincushions
Unit 4
Taverham Crafts
Taverham Nursery Centre
Fir Covert Road
Taverham
Norwich NR8 6HT

Loricraft
4 Big Lane
Lambourn
Berkshire

Needlestyle
5 The Woolmead
Farnham
Surrey GU9 7TX

Needlestyle
24–26 West Street
Alresford
Hampshire

Needlework
Ann Bartleet
Bucklers Farm
Coggeshall
Essex CO6 1SB

Needle and Thread
80 High Street
Horsell
Woking
Surrey GU21 4SZ

The Needlewoman
21 Needles Alley
off New Street
Birmingham B2 5AE

T. Parker
124 Corhampton Road
Boscombe East
Bournemouth
Dorset BH6 5NZ

Jane Playford
North Lodge
Church Close
West Runton
Norfolk NR27 9QY

Redburn Crafts
Squires Garden Centre
Halliford Road
Upper Halliford
Shepperton
Middlesex TW17 8RU

Christine Riley
53 Barclay Street
Stonehaven
Kincardineshire
Scotland

Peter & Beverley Scarlett
Strupak
Hill Head
Cold Wells
Ellon
Grampian
Scotland

Ken & Pat Schultz
134 Wisbech Road
Thornley
Peterborough

J. S. Sear
Lacecraft Supplies
8 Hillview
Sherington
Buckinghamshire MK16
 9NJ

Sebalace
Waterloo Mills
Howden Road
Silsden
West Yorkshire BD2
 0NA

A. Sells
49 Pedley Lane
Clifton
Shefford
Bedfordshire

Shireburn Lace
Finkle Court
Finkle Hill
Sherburn in Elmet
North Yorkshire LS25
 6EB

SMP
4 Garners Close
Chalfont St Peter
Buckinghamshire SL9
 0HB

Southern Handicrafts
20 Kensington Gardens
Brighton
Sussex BN1 4AC

Spangles
Carole Morris
Cashburn Lane
Burwell
Cambridgeshire CB5 0ED

Stitchery
Finkle Street
Richmond
North Yorkshire

Stitches
Dovehouse Shopping
 Parade
Warwick Road
Olton
Solihull
West Midlands

Teazle Embroideries
35 Boothferry Road
Hull
North Humberside

Lynn Turner
Church Meadow Crafts
15 Carisbrooke Drive
Winsford
Cheshire CW7 1LN

The Craft House
23 Bar Street
Scarborough
North Yorkshire

George Walker
The Corner Shop
Rickinghall
Diss
Norfolk

West End Lace Supplies
Ravensworth Court Road
Mortimer West End
Reading
Berkshire RG7 3UD

George White
  Lacemakers' Supplies
40 Heath Drive
Boston Spa
West Yorkshire L23 6PB

Bobbins

A. R. Archer
The Poplars
Shetland
near Stowmarket
Suffolk IP14 3DE

Bartlett, Caesar and
  Partners
12 Creslow Court
Stony Stratford
Milton Keynes MK11
  1NN
  also at:
The Glen
Shorefield Road
Downton
Lymington
Hampshire SO41 0LH

T. Brown
Temple Lane Cottage
Littledean
Cinderford
Gloucestershire

Bryncraft Bobbins
B. J. Phillips
Pantglas
Cellan
Lampeter
Dyfed SA48 BJD

Chrisken Bobbins
26 Cedar Drive
Kingsclere
Buckinghamshire RG15
  8TD

Malcolm J. Fielding
2 Northern Terrace
Moss Lane
Silverdale
Lancashire LA5 0ST

Richard Gravestock
Highwood
Crews Hill
Alfrick
Worcestershire WR6
  5HF

Larkfield Crafts
Hilary Ricketts
4 Island Cottages
Mapledurwell
Basingstoke
Hampshire RG25 2LU

Loricraft
4 Big Lane
Lambourn
Berkshire

T. Parker
124 Corhampton Road
Boscombe East
Bournemouth
Dorset BH6 5NZ

D. H. Shaw
47 Lamor Crescent
Thrushcroft
Rotherham
South Yorkshire S66
  9QD

Sizelands
1 Highfield Road
Winslow
Buckinghamshire MK10
  3QU

Christine & David
  Springett
21 Hillmorton Road
Rugby
Warwickshire CV22 5DF

Richard Viney
Unit 7
Port Royal Street
Southsea
Hampshire PO5 3UD

West End Lace Suppliers
Ravensworth Court Road
Mortimer West End
Reading
Berkshire RG7 3UD

Lace pillows

Newnham Lace
  Equipment
15 Marlowe Close
Basingstoke
Hampshire RG24 9DD

Bartlett, Caesar and
  Partners
12 Creslow Court
Stony Stratford
Milton Keynes MK11
  1NN
  also at:
The Glen
Shorefield Road
Downton
Lymington
Hampshire SO41 0LH

Silk embroidery and lace thread

E. & J. Piper
Silverlea
Flax Lane
Glemsford
Suffolk CO10 7RS

Silk weaving yarn

Hilary Chetwynd
Kipping Cottage
Cheriton
Alresford
Hampshire SO24 0PW

Frames and mounts

Doreen Campbell
Highcliff
Bremiham Road
Malmesbury
Wiltshire

Matt coloured transparent adhesive film

Heffers Graphic Shop
26 King Street
Cambridge CB1 1LN

Linen by the metre (yard) and made up articles of church linen

Mary Collins
Church Furnishings
St Andrew's Hall
Humber Doucy Lane
Ipswich
Suffolk IP4 3BP

Hayes & Finch
Head Office & Factory
Hanson Road
Aintree
Liverpool L9 9BP

UNITED STATES OF AMERICA

Arbor House
22 Arbor Lane
Roslyn Hights, NY 11577

Baltazor Inc.
3262 Severn Avenue
Metairie, LA 7002

Beggars' Lace
P.O. Box 17263
Denver, Colo. 80217

Berga Ullman Inc.
P.O. Box 918
North Adams, MA 01247

Frederick J. Fawcett
129 South Street
Boston, MA 02130

Frivolité
15526 Densmore N.
Seattle, WA 98113

Happy Hands
3007 S.W. Marshall
Pendleton, Oreg. 97180

International Old Lacers
P.O. Box 1029
Westminster, Colo.
  80030

Lace Place de Belgique
800 S.W. 17th Street
Boca Raton, FL 33432

Lacis
2150 Stuart Street
Berkeley, CA 9470

Robin's Bobbins
RTL Box 1736
Mineral Bluff, GA 30559

Robin and Russ
Handweavers
533 North Adams Street
McMinnvills, Oreg.
 97128

Some Place
2990 Adline Street
Berkeley, CA 94703

Osma G. Todd Studio
319 Mendoza Avenue
Coral Gables, FL 33134

The Unique And Art
 Lace Cleaners
5926 Delman Boulevard
St Louis, MO 63112

Van Scriver Bobbin Lace
130 Cascadilla Park
Ithaca, NY 14850

The World in Stitches
82 South Street
Milford, NH 03055

AUSTRALIA

Australian Lace magazine
P.O. Box 1291
Toowong
Queensland 4066

Dentelles Lace Supplies
c/o Betty Franks
39 Lang Terrace
Northgate 4013
Brisbane
Queensland

The Lacemaker
94 Fordham Avenue
Hartwell
Victoria 3124

Spindle and Loom
Arcade 83
Longueville Road
Lane Cove
NSW 2066

Tulis Crafts
201 Avoca Street
Randwick
NSW 2031

BELGIUM

't Handwerkhuisje
Katelijnestraat 23
8000 Bruges

Kantcentrum
Balstraat 14
8000 Bruges

Manufacture Belge de
 Dentelle
6 Galerie de la Reine
Galeries Royales St
 Hubert
1000 Bruxelles

Orchidée
Mariastraat 18
8000 Bruges

Ann Thys
't Apostelientje
Balstraat 11
8000 Bruges

FRANCE

Centre d'Initiations à la
 Dentelle du Puy
2 Rue Duguesclin
43000 Le Puy en Velay

A L'Econome
Anne-Marie Deydier
Ecole de Dentelle aux
 Fuseaux
10 rue Paul Chenavard
69001 Lyon

Rougier and Plé
13–15 bd des Filles de
 Calvaire
75003 Paris

GERMANY

Der Fenster Laden
Berliner Str. 8
D6483 Bad Soden
Salmünster

P. P. Hempel
Ortolanweg 34
1000 Berlin 47

HOLLAND

Blokker's Boektiek
Bronsteeweg 4/4a
2101 AC Heemstede

Heikina De Ruijter
Zuiderstraat 1
9693 ER Nieuweschans

Theo Brejaart
Postbus 5199
3008 AD Rotterdam

Magazijn *De Vlijt*
Lijnmarkt 48
Utrecht

SWITZERLAND

Fadehax
Inh. Irene Solca
4105 Biel-Benken
Basel

NEW ZEALAND

Peter McLeavey
P.O. Box 69.007
Auckland 8

SOURCES OF INFORMATION

The Lace Guild
The Hollies
53 Audnam
Stourbridge
West Midlands DY8 4AE

The Lacemakers' Circle
49 Wardwick
Derby DE1 1 HY

The Lace Society
Linwood
Stratford Road
Oversley
Alcester
Warwickshire BY9 6PG

The British College of
 Lace
21 Hillmorton Road
Rugby
Warwickshire CV22 5DF

The English Lace School
Oak House
Church Stile
Woodbury
Nr Exeter
Devon

United Kingdom Director
 of International Old
 Lacers
S. Hurst
4 Dollius Road
London N3 1RG

Ring of Tatters
Mrs C. Appleton
Nonesuch
5 Ryeland Road
Ellerby
Saltburn by Sea
Cleveland TS13 5LP

UNITED STATES

International Old Lacers
President
Gunvor Jorgensen
366 Bradley Avenue
Northvale, NJ 076647

BOOK SUPPLIERS

The following are stockists of the complete Batsford/Dryad Press range:

Avon

Bridge Bookshop
7 Bridge Street
Bath BA2 4AS

Waterstone & Co.
4–5 Milsom Street
Bath BA1 1DA

Bedfordshire

Arthur Sells
Lane Cove
49 Pedley Lane
Clifton
Shefford SG17 5QT

Berkshire

Loricraft
4 Big Lane
Lambourn

West End Lace Supplies
Ravensworth Court Road
Mortimer West End
Reading RG7 3UD

Buckinghamshire

J. S. Sear Lacecraft
  Supplies
8 Hillview
Sherington MK16 9NJ

Cambridgeshire

Dillons The Bookstore
Sidney Street
Cambridge

Cheshire

Lyn Turner
Church Meadow Crafts
15 Carisbrook Drive
Winsford

Cornwall

Creative Books
22A River Street
Truro TR1 2SJ

Devon

Creative Crafts &
  Needlework
18 High Street
Totnes TQ9 5NP

Honiton Lace Shop
44 High Street
Honiton EX14 8PJ

Dorset

F. Herring & Sons
High West Street
Dorchester DT1 1UP

Tim Parker (mail order)
124 Corhampton Road
Boscombe East
Bournemouth BH6 5NL

Christopher Williams
19 Morrison Avenue
Parkstone
Poole BH17 4AD

Durham

Lacemaid
6, 10 & 15 Stoneybeck
Bishop Middleham
County Durham DL17
  9BL

Gloucestershire

Southgate Handicrafts
68 Southgate Street
Gloucester GL1 1TX

Waterstone & Co.
89–90 The Promenade
Cheltenham GL50 1NB

Hampshire

Creative Crafts
11 The Square
Winchester
SO23 9ES

Doreen Gill
14 Barnfield Road
Petersfield GU31 4DR

Larkfield Crafts
4 Island Cottages
Mapledurwell
Basingstoke RG23 2LU

Needlestyle
24–26 West Street
Alresford

Ruskins
27 Bell Street
Romsey

Isle of Wight

Busy Bobbins
Unit 7
Scarrots Lane
Newport PO30 1JD

Kent

The Handicraft Shop
47 Northgate
Canterbury

Hatchards
The Great Hall
Mount Pleasant Road
Tunbridge Wells

London

W. & G. Foyles Ltd
119 Charing Cross Road
  WC2H 0EB

Hatchards
187 Piccadilly W1

Middlesex

Redburn Crafts
Squires Garden Centre
Halliford Road
Upper Halliford
Shepperton TW17 8RU

Norfolk

Alby Lace Museum
Cromer Road
Alby
Norwich NR11 7QE

Jane's Pincushions
Taverham Craft Unit 4
Taverham Nursery Centre
Fir Covert Road
Taverham
Norwich NR8 6HT

Waterstone & Co.
30 London Street
Norwich NR2 1LD

Northamptonshire

D. J. Hornsby
149 High Street
Burton Latimer
Kettering NN15 SRL

Scotland

Embroidery Shop
51 William Street
Edinburgh
Lothian EH3 7LW

Waterstone & Co.
236 Union Street
Aberdeen AB1 1TN

Somerset

Bridge Bookshop
62 Bridge Street
Taunton TA1 1UD

Staffordshire

J. & J. Ford
October Hill
65 Upper Way
Upper Longdon
Rugeley WS16 1QB

Sussex

Waterstone & Co.
120 Terminus Road
Eastbourne

Warwickshire

C. & D. Springett
21 Hillmorton Road
Rugby CV22 6DF

Wiltshire

Everyman Bookshop
5 Bridge Street
Salisbury SP1 2ND

North Yorkshire

Craft Basics
9 Gillygate
York

Shireburn Lace
Finkle Court
Finkle Hill
Sherburn in Elmet LS25
   6EA

The Craft House
23 Bar Street
Scarborough

Wales (mail order)

Bryncraft Bobbins
B. J. Phillips
Pantglas
Cellan
Lampeter
Dyfed SA48 BJD

West Midlands

Needlewoman
Needles Alley
off New Street
Birmingham

West Yorkshire

Sebalace
Waterloo Mill
Howden Road
Silsden BD20 0HA

George White
   Lacemaking Supplies
40 Heath Drive
Boston Spa LS23 6PB

Jo Firth
58 Kent Crescent
Lowtown
Pudsey
Leeds LS28 9EB

TRANSLATION OF LACE TERMS

English	Dutch	French	German
adding a pair	een paar inleggen	ajouter une paire	ein neues Paar einhängen
back stitch	zeuren aan de binnen kant	rabacher à l'interieur	
bobbin	klos	fuseau	Klöppel
braid/tape	bandje	galon	Band
changing	wisseltje	changement	Wechsel
cloth stitch	linnenslag	mat	Leinenschlag
crossing	kruisen	croiser	kreuzen
double stitch	hele slag/dubbele netslag	double-grillé	Ganz *oder* Gitterschlag
fillings	vullingen	fonds de remplissage	Füllungen
four about the pin	(rechte) randslag	changement de meneurs d'un côté la paire derrière l'épingle	Randschlag
footside	zelfkant	lisière le pied	echter Randschlag
gimp	dikke draad	cordonnet	Konturfaden
ground	grond	fond	Grund
half stitch	netslag/halve slag	le point grillé	Halbschlag
knot	knoop	noeud	Knoten
loop	lusje	ganse	Schlinge
motif	motief	rempli	Motiv
outer edge/headside	buitenrand	côté extérieur	Aussenrand
pair	paar	paire	Paar
passive pair	hangend paar	traversiers	Hängepaar
pattern	patroon	carton	Klöppelbrief
picot	picot	pionton	Zänkelchen
pin	speld	épingle	Stecknadel
pinhole	speldegat	trou d'épingle	Stechnadelloch
pivot	krulbewerking	pivotement	Kräuseln
plait	vlecht	corde de 4 fuseaux	Flechter
false plait	valse vlecht	corde fausse	fälsche Flechter
raised/rolled	reliëf	relief	Relief
scallop edge	geschulpte buitenrand	coquille	muschelförmiger Aussenrand
scroll	krul	volute	Schnörkel
setting up	opzetten	montage	aufhängen
sewing out	afhechten	crocheter	zusammenhäkeln
sewing	aanhaken	accrocher	anhäkeln
snowflakes	sneeuwvlokken	floçons de neige	Schneeflocken

English	Dutch	French	German
stitch	slag	point	Schlag
tally/leadwork	vormslag	point d'esprit	Formschlag
thread	draad/garen	fil	Faden
throw out a pair	een paar uitleggen	ôter une paire	auslegen eines Paares
twist	draaien	tourner	drehen
tying off	afknopen	nouer	verknüpfen
Valenciennes ground	vierkante maas	maille carrée	quadritische Masche
vein	nerf	grain	Nerv
windmill	molen	moulin	Mühle
workers	lopend paar	meneurs	Läuferpaar
working directions	werkwijze	méthode de travail	arbeitsweise

crochet	haken	crochet	Spitzen
chain	losse	chainette	Luftmaschen
double	vaste	maille serrée	feste Masche
double treble	dubbel stokje	double-bride	doppel Stäbchen
half treble	half stokje	demi-bride	
hook	haaknaald	un crochet en acier	Garnhäkelnadel
picot	picot	picot	Pikot
slip stitch	halve vaste	maille coulée	Kettmasche
treble	stokje	bride	Stäbchen

tatting	frivolité		
chain	boog	chainette	
double stitch	verbinden	double point	
loop	lus	bouch	Schlinge
picot	picot	picot	Pikot
ring	ringen	cercle	
shuttle	spoeltje/schuitje	navette	

FURTHER READING

Bruges Flower Lace: Edna Sutton (Batsford, 1986)

Carrickmacross Lace: Nellie O'Cleirigh (Dryad, 1985)

Creative Design in Needlepoint Lace: Nina Lovesey (Batsford, 1983)

Designing for Bruges Flower Lace: Edna Sutton (Batsford, 1987)

Duchesse: Jose van Pamelen-Hagenaars (Drukkerig-Uipgeverij Pieters BV, 1983)

Introduction to Needlepoint Lace: Nina Lovesey (Batsford, 1985)

Manual of Bobbin Lacemaking: Margaret Maidment (Pitman & Sons 1931, Paul B. Minet, 1971)

Syllabus Binche I: Anne-Marie Verbeke-Billiet (Drukkerig van den Broele Bruge, 1988)

Syllabus Binche II: Anne-Marie Verbeke-Billiet (as above)

Technique of Needlepoint Lace: Nina Lovesey (Batsford, 1980)

Valenciennes Variatiis: Yvonne Krijsman & Margaret Dirksen

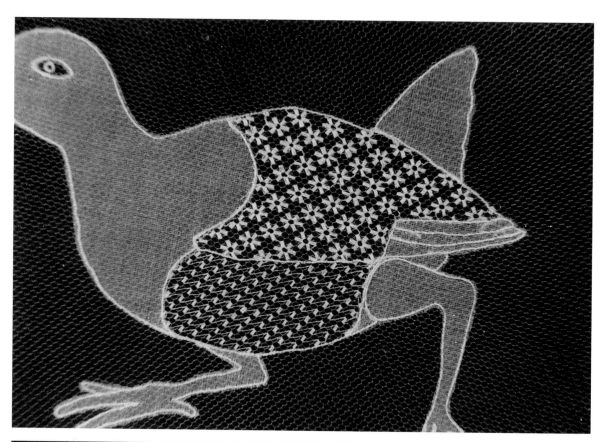

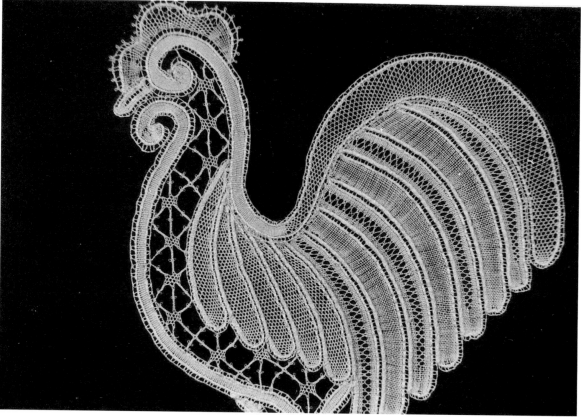

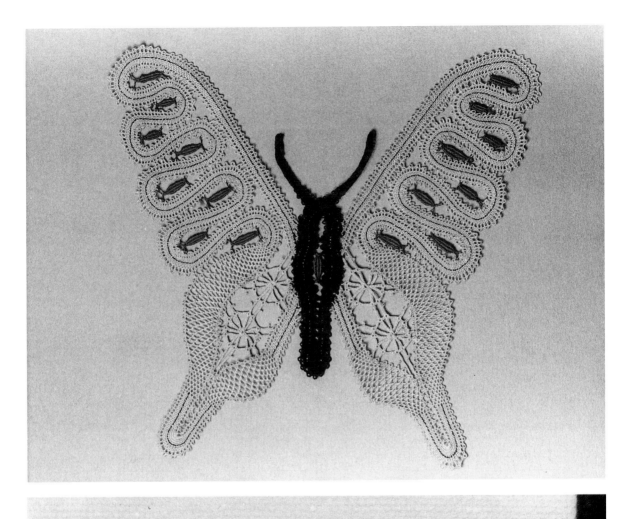

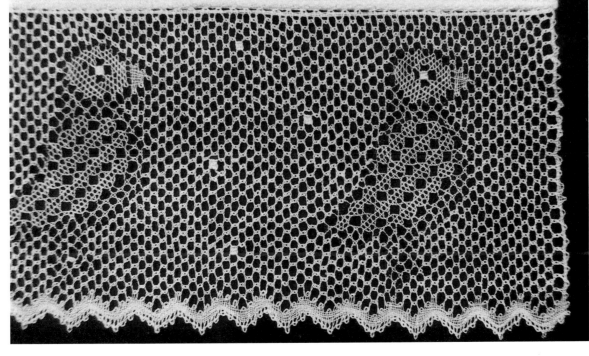